ERICH BAUER

HOROSCOPE 2024

In the glow of the sun

Imprint
Publisher
Masterbrain GmbH, Roseggerweg 148
A-8044 Graz, Austria
Independently published
info@masterbrain.com
Illustrations, graphics: Adobe Stock
Photos Erich Bauer: Werner Krug
Author: Erich Bauer
Layout & Cover: Elisabeth Koch, MBA

TABLE OF CONTENTS

2024 HOROSCOPE

In the glow of the sun

Welcome to the mystical world of the year 2024, ruled by the majestic Sun. All other planets must bend to its will, because its rays are of great importance for our future. When we think of the sun, summer immediately appears in our mind's eye, with its sun-drenched days and the opportunity to enjoy nature. We see flowering meadows where golden blossoms vie for our attention and trees adorning the blue sky as if for a festive wedding.

But the sun also has a dark side that we will encounter in 2024. Autumn and winter will remind us that not everything can always be radiant and beautiful. The sun has two faces, and we will get to know both. But be reassured, because we will not be predominantly afflicted by unpleasant influences. The coming year will bring us a balanced mixture. Half positive, half negative. We should always keep this realization in mind when we are in difficult times. Because these will not last.

In addition, the relationship of the other planets to the Sun plays an important role. Especially the slow planets that stay in the same zodiac sign throughout the year have an influence on us. Jupiter, Saturn, Uranus, Neptune and Pluto belong to this category. Let's take a closer look at Pluto, which for some time has been viewed critically by astrologers and clairvoyants. Problems and even crises are often attributed to it. On Januaryy 21, Pluto enters the zodiac sign Aquarius, where it will stay for the next 15 years after a short break in autumn. Pluto represents the principle of transience and brings transformations. Aquarius is about renewal, improvement, invention, self-design and idealism. Pluto could also bring unpleasant events such as uprisings and revolutions. It reMayns exciting.

Neptune stays the whole year in the zodiac sign of Pisces, which from an astrological point of view stands for peace. This peace comes when we do not fixate too much on externals, but on inner values. More and more people could start meditating, for example. Saturn is also in the zodiac sign of Pisces throughout the year. Normally Saturn ensures order, but in the sign of Pisces it is no longer so strong. This means that institutions that provide order could become weaker, while others, such as churches, become more important. Exactly how this will affect each individual cannot be predicted. However, we can hope that Saturn will work in the same direction as Neptune and support the path to meditation.

Uranus lingers in the zodiac sign of Taurus, where it has already spent the last two years. Uranus brings Aquarian energy that aims to make the world more human. Ultimately, this could mean that money in general becomes less important. Of course, this is an illusion, but there will be changes in this direction.

Jupiter stays in the zodiac sign Taurus until May 25, which means that not much will change for the time being from an astrological point of view. But then Jupiter enters the zodiac sign Gemini and opens doors and gates for change.

You are certainly wondering what all this means for you. The answer to this is individual for everyone. Learn more about your zodiac sign on the following pages. Here's some more advice for everyone, regardless of your zodiac sign: Troubled times are ahead. But there is an astrological answer to this, namely not to let yourself be guided too much by external influences. We are fortunate that Neptune is in the zodiac sign of Pisces. This opens a door into a world where we can find security. All we have to do is close our eyes, feel inside ourselves and give thanks.

Yours sincerely, Erich Bauer

PISCES
(February 20-March 20)

The sun sets the tone in 2024. For you, this is good fortune. Because there is a good relationship between it and your zodiac sign Pisces, so you benefit directly from its reign. You can be quite sure, it will never be really unpleasant in 2024. There is always a way out - even if things get difficult. Saturn is in your zodiac sign throughout the year. This is equivalent to this planet taking a break and leaving you alone with it. In the very first place, it means that your life becomes easier. You have less stress, your work is manageable, can be done without overtime, and you also do not always have to do everything alone, but get help and support from everywhere. However, this also requires that you "play along". What is meant is that you also allow yourself more rest and relaxation. It could also be that you are worrying and trying all the harder. That would be quite wrong. You are absolved in 2024, allowed to let yourself go. Neptune is also in your zodiac sign. It has been there for the last three years. But only now, through the presence of Saturn, he is really close for you. This opens a door into the realm of mysticism. No one else will find it easier now. You only need to take a little time, close your eyes, get involved in the moment, and you will experience the happiness that is more beautiful than anything else. Participation in the mystical world also enriches your everyday life. You have more confidence and feel safe. Dive problems also, Pull yourself back into your world of mysticism.

LOVE

Surely you know that your zodiac sign is "Pisces-e", plural, plural. This is to be taken as an indication that you have two sides in you, a "yes" and a "no". For example, you long with your whole being for a fulfilled love, a close partnership and are ready to give up your own self for it. But the "no" is just as strong, even if it is not always clearly audible. In the year of

7

the Sun, that is 2024, you experience a love that fulfills both your sides: Devotion and independence, commitment and freedom. Single meet a being who loves you as you are with all your beauties and also the little "quirks". Yes, it is even the case that it is precisely the small inconsistencies and contradictions that strengthen the fire of love. Couples experience a harmony and understanding that has not been seen for a long time. Singles are also being generously taken care of. You are becoming a little more gentle. This is exactly what increases your popularity. Don't resent it if Jupiter now also gives you a little lesson along the way. It is well meant: you are a totally lovable woman. The remark in certain astro books that you are cool or even undercooled is nonsense. But you often don't give the other person the space he needs to get really warm. If you sometimes become more wait-and-see and passive here, your love will benefit enormously in the solar year 2024, and you certainly won't end it as a single.

Starry magic:
Enigmatic, soulful,
mystical, successful

CAREER

There is an exciting meeting between Uranus and Jupiter in the spring. This looks like a seed will sprout within you. This may relate to a promotion at work or a new job that you enjoy more. It is also possible that this refers to a person coming into your life and enriching it. Exact or even concrete details are not revealed. Saturn in your zodiac sign is hatching something for you. Maybe this doesn't suit you, if you don't know what's coming up. But you will have to get used to that. Because Neptune is also in your zodiac sign. There you will stand in the coming year again and again before riddles or a question mark. Then you need trust. The cosmos will definitely not let you down in 2024. On the contrary, it takes you by the hand and leads you on the right way. If you are no longer working, the aspect that has already been mentioned, namely the conjunction between Uranus and Jupiter, comes into play for you. No matter how old you are, do not put your hands in your lap, but throw yourself into a new activity. This can be a hobby or further education, for example, in an adult education course.

CHARACTER:	Introverted, idealistic, selfless
PERSONAL APPEARANCE:	Enigmatic, reserved
FEELING:	Intimate, soulful
STONE:	Opal
ANIMAL:	Dolphin
FLOWER:	Poppy
BEST DAY:	Friday

JANUARY

♥ **Love** You will feel moments of happiness in love. There are three reasons for this. Saturn and Neptune in your zodiac sign mean you are with yourself, in your center. This creates independence. You don't need a partner to cuddle you, you are doing well on your own. There is also Jupiter. He makes you radiate because you are so happy yourself. And Mars helps you radiate self-confidence.

🏆 **Success** A new era can begin! Erase negative experiences, setbacks, disappointments, bad luck, in the worst case bankruptcies from your memory. That was once! In 2024 you will find yourself, suddenly know exactly where your strengths lie and feel called. This is really a phase in which the scales fall from your eyes and you see everything more clearly.

👍 **Good for** The year is ripe for a project that will bring you and your partner together.

☹ **Bad for** Pinching is punished by Saturn with the red card

✦ **The best star partners** Cancer, Virgo

Energy level Pisces: January 2024

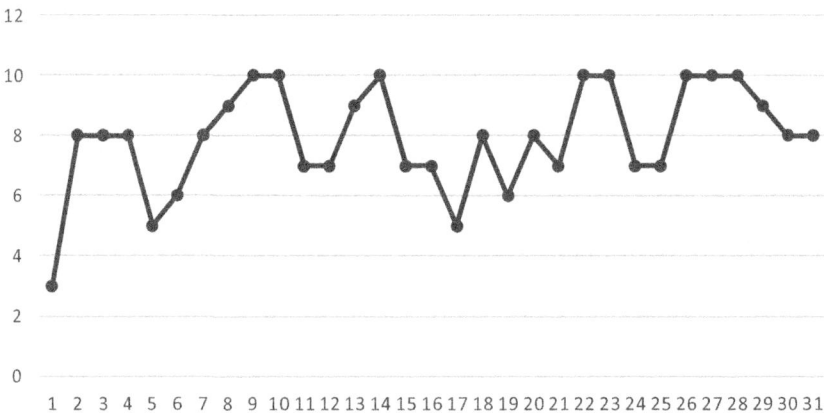

FEBRUARY

Now Pluto is in the zodiac sign Aquarius, where it will stay for almost 20 years. So it's certainly not wrong to get ready for it now: Pluto demands change. It means letting go of habits to make way for something new and better.

💜 *Love* Februaryy is a wonderful month to strengthen your love. This does not require big gifts, but simply that you show your heart. Then in the second half of the month something completely different can happen, namely that you become jealous.

🏆 *Success* Routine is boring and does not lead to extra money. If you want to win, you must be ready to dare something. But at the same time, the stars proclaimed that you should not go too far out on a limb. Difficult, isn't it?

👍 *Good for* Spending less money

☹ *Bad for* Letting it hang out

✦ *Best star partners* Taurus, Cancer, Virgo

Energy level Pisces: February 2024

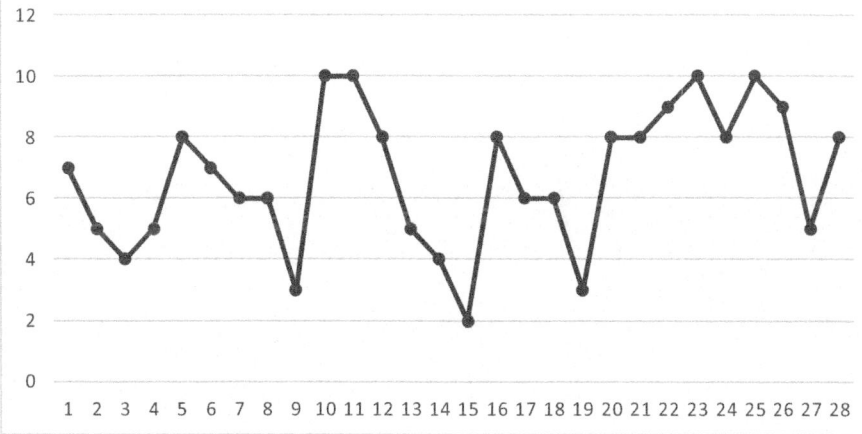

MARCH

♥ *Love* Venus is in your zodiac sign from March 12, and on the 23rd Mars comes and hooks up with her. This can only mean that love will fall from the sky. You are truly the luckiest sign of the zodiac among all. You can experience dreamy hours, with your current partner or - if you are currently single - with your new one.

♕ *Success* In terms of career, you are ambitious, super-committed and ready for any leap upwards.

If you have to choose between an enjoyable evening with your sweetheart and a team meeting deep into the night, you therefore tend to choose the latter. Blame Mercury and really good positions from Jupiter, Saturn and Pluto. Your commitment will pay off in the truest sense of the word. Expect to make more money.

👍 *Good for* Self-overcoming bad

☹ *Bad for* Ego

✦ *Best star partners* Capricorn

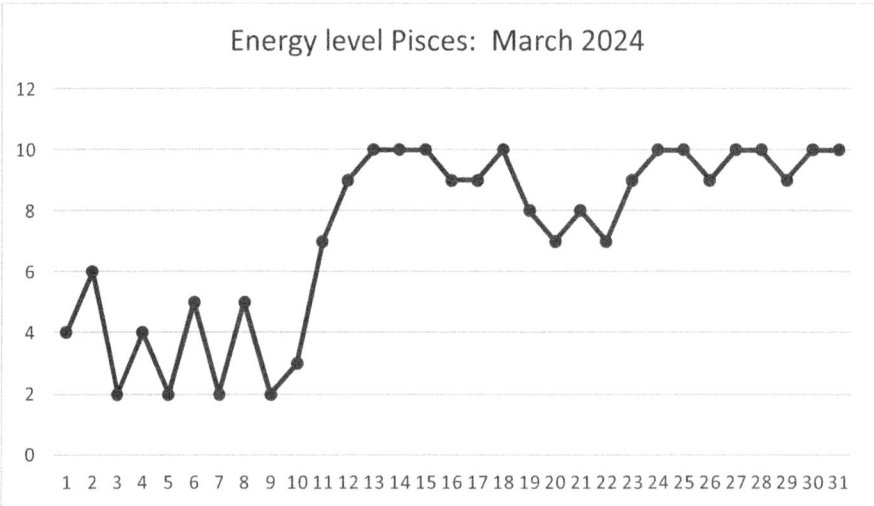

Energy level Pisces: March 2024

APRIL

💜 **Love** Mars is in your zodiac sign and takes care of you. This is almost like a guarantee to meet someone who will stir your insides. Best dating time is around the New Moon on the 8th and then again at the Full Moon on April 23.

🏆 **Success** Saturn and Mars are in your sign Pisces. Their message: work less, but have more time for the finer things in life. Of course, this doesn't always work out. But you will certainly get into situations where you may choose one (stress) or the other (relaxation).

👍 **Good for** Your finances

☹ **Bad for** Hold back from deals that aren't sound

✦ **Best star partners** Capricorn, Virgo

Energy level Pisces: April 2024

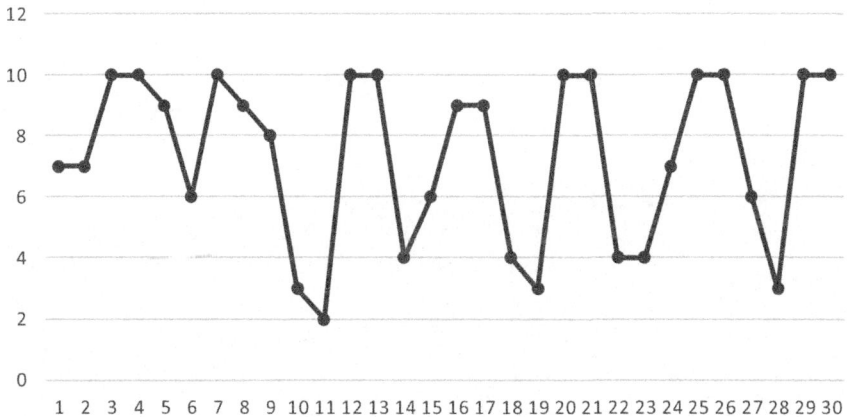

MAY

♥ *Love* The love planet Venus is very favorable for most of the month. This gives you more charm and more desire. It is quite possible that you will have an experience in May that will make you happy. In the second half of the month the Sun and Jupiter meet. This gives you the power of persuasion.

♙ *Success* You have great stars and can advance your life's work, push yourself to the forefront, ask for more money, get married, move into a new apartment. Everything you have accomplished so far can be secured. However, after the 20th of the month you should refrain from new initiatives. Now it is important that you allow yourself rest and relaxation.

👍 *Good for* Sorting out problems.

☹ *Bad for* Not taking care of your health!

✦ *Best star partners* Virgo

Energy level Pisces: May 2024

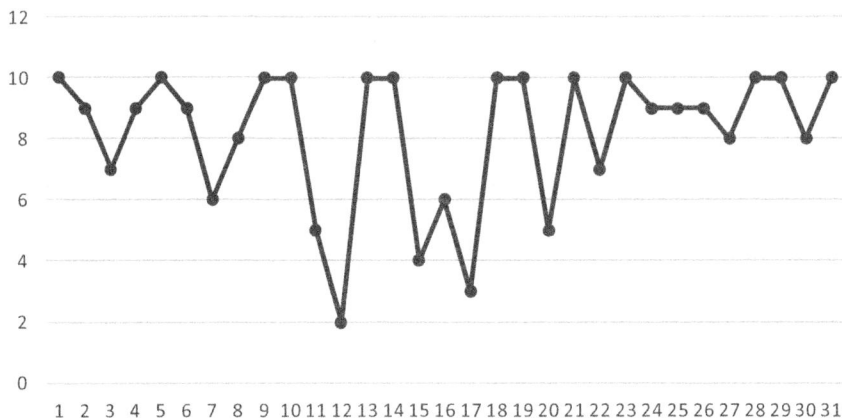

14

JUNE

💜 **Love** From June 10, Mars moves into a position that gives you the security to trust your feelings even more, to let yourself fall. And the stars say, at the latest on the 17th of the month Venus takes a position that says: there are strong arms catching you. Maybe you'll be especially lucky, and these arms will belong to a Virgo. Then everything would be fine.

🏆 **Success** Saturn is in the zodiac sign of Pisces. There you are confronted with a task where others give up. But you rise above yourself and create a positive result. However, also take into account the planet Uranus, which is in sextile to your zodiac sign. There is basically always to expect that something unexpected life happens.

👍 **Good for** More opportunities in business

☹ **Bad for** Caution, Mars also makes you overconfident.

✦ **Best star partners** Aries, Cancer, Virgo, Taurus

Energy level Pisces: June 2024

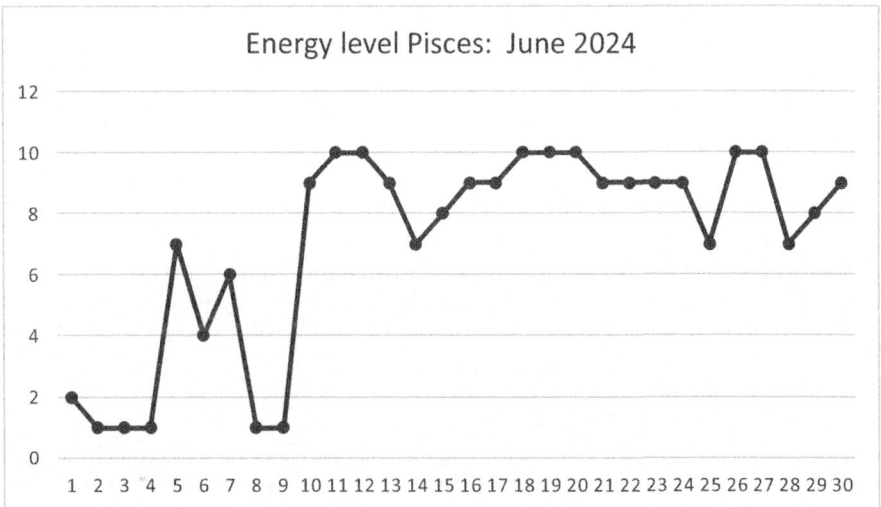

JULY

💜 **Love** The Sun and Venus are in your 5th solar house until mid-month, which has always been considered a sign of happy unions in astrology. You can bet that Pisces will be marching to the registry office in heaps now. And, of course, the love rate in your partnership increases.

🏆 **Success** Saturn is especially strong in July. He is in your zodiac sign. Normally you fear him. It is often said in astrology that when this star enters your star sign, there are troubles and plagues associated with it. Often this is the case. But not with you. You may even relax, and still everything goes your way.

👍 **Good for** Love like in fairy tales

☹ **Bad for** Frivolity

✦ **Best star partners** Taurus, Capricorn, Pisces

Energy level Pisces: July 2024

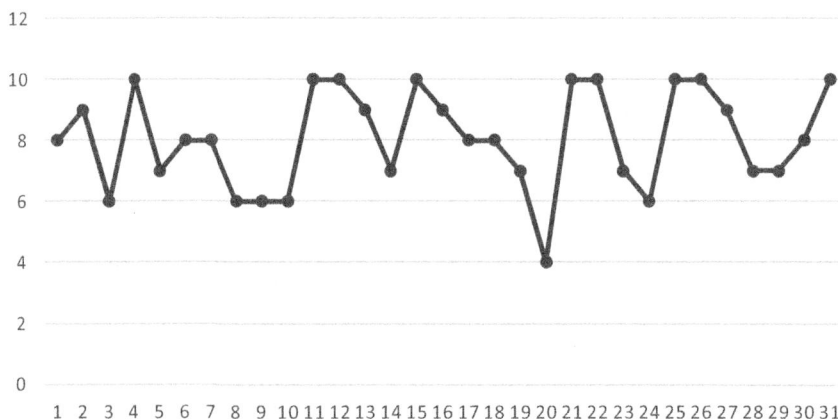

AUGUST

💜 **Love** You tried very hard to please everyone and everything. Not infrequently you were disappointed. The consequence of this - Saturn, which is in your zodiac sign, is responsible for this - is a small but groundbreaking change: you become more relaxed in August, are closest to yourself without neglecting your counterpart.

🏆 **Success** In astrology Saturn does not have a particularly good reputation. It slows you down, restricts you, creates problems. In your case, Saturn comes as a friend. As a result, you begin to commit and specialize. Therefore, invest time and money in further education, attend seminars, courses, learn in your field.

👍 **Good for** Egoism

☹ **Bad for** Anxiety

✨ **Best star partners** Leo, Aquarius

Energy level Pisces: August 2024

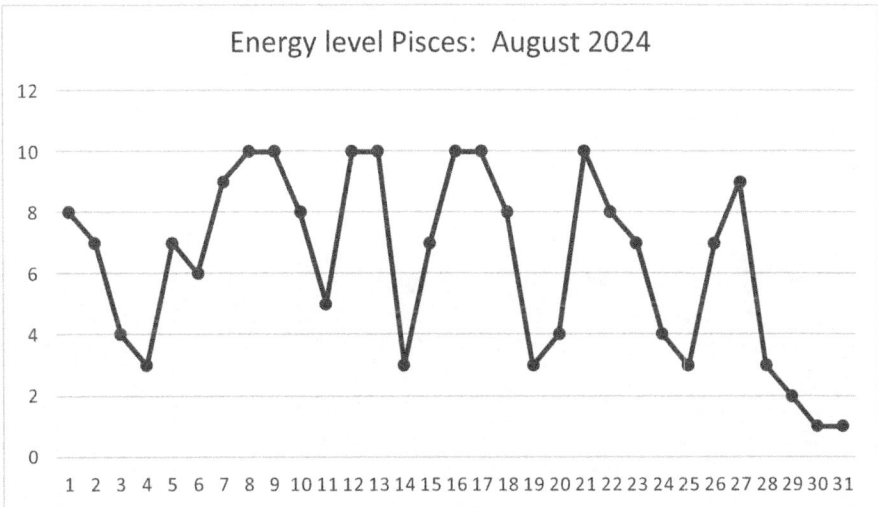

SEPTEMBER

❤️ **Love** With the Sun opposite your star sign in Virgo, you move mountains. Sounds like a home game with a guarantee of success? Yes, if you consider the following: Time and again Neptune interferes in a disruptive way. You sometimes give people too much trust, are naive and overly nice and optimistic.

🏆 **Success** Success, happiness and satisfaction don't come over-night. Not in September. Rather, in slices. You are caught up in yourself and talk yourself out of economic crisis or overall situation. But if you connect with Saturn, forces grow, the ego strengthens, first ideas and visions take root.

👍 **Good for** Togetherness

☹ **Bad for** Loneliness

✦ **Best star partners** Pisces, Virgo, Cancer, Capricorn

Energy level Pisces: September 2024

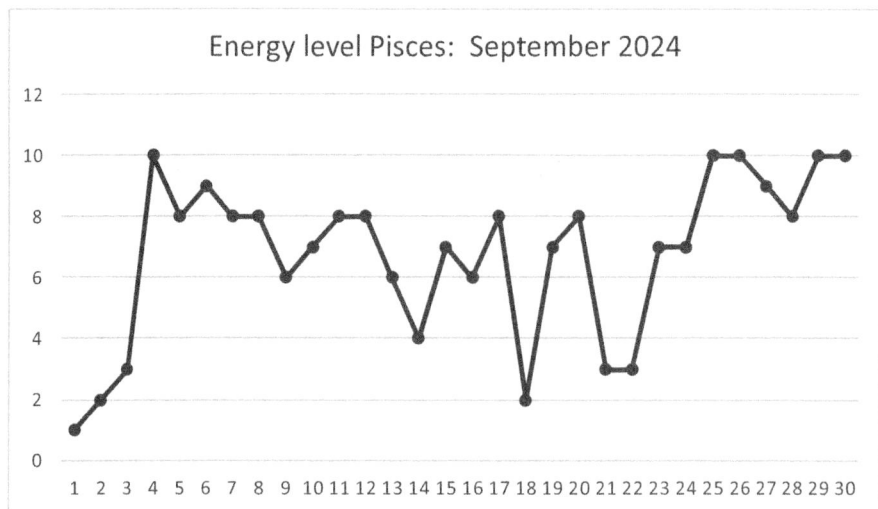

OCTOBER

💜 *Love* You are experiencing a springtime of love in the middle of autumn. This is because now the planets Mars and Venus are after you and making love palatable. A particularly promising time runs right into the first week of October. There Mars and Venus shake hands. .

🏆 *Success* However, business also plays a role. Here it is important that you do not let yourself be frightened by existential worries; you tend to be a bit of a doomsayer. Therefore, chase away gloomy thoughts, distract yourself, cheer up! This is especially true for the time around the full moon on October 17.

👍 *Good for* Friendship

☹ *Bad for* Illusions

✦ *Best star partners* Leo, Aquarius, Capricorn

Energy level Pisces: October 2024

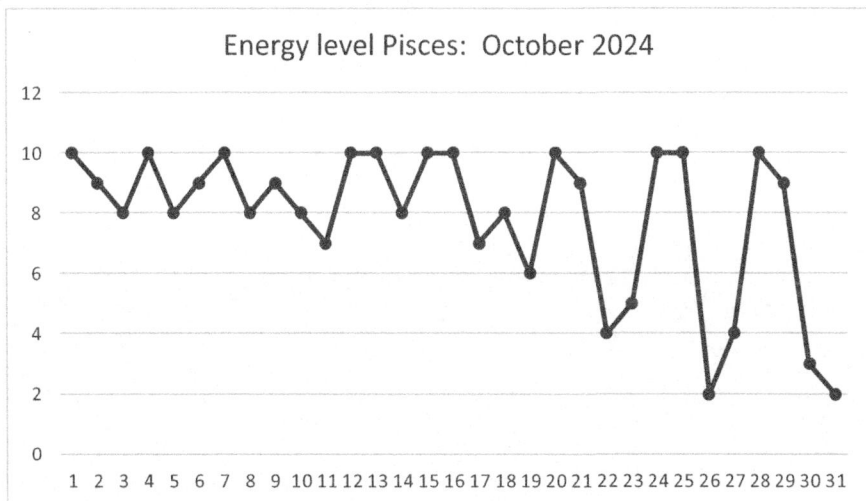

NOVEMBER

💜 **Love** From about the 12th of the month you are the darling of the stars and get the chance to have a wonderful time. You may let yourself drift and give in to all emotions: the passionate, the tender, the possessive, the yearning.

🏆 **Success** Your strongest time begins on March 12: 90 percent of all celestial forces are behind you, threading encounters of fate. You may meet your future boss or a be-nefactor who will take away your money worries. But do not try to force anything! Either it happens by itself or the thing is no good for you: Inshallah, that's the way it is with fish!

👍 **Good for** Partnership

☹ **Bad for** Being coward

✦ **Best star partners** Pisces, Virgo

Energy level Pisces: November 2024

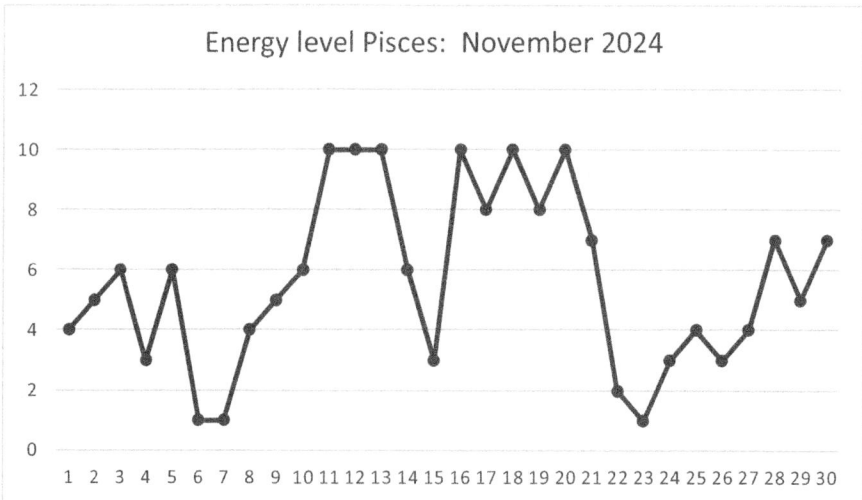

DECEMBER

♥ **Love** You have dream prospects with the opposite sex on the first days of December, you are relaxed, charming, cheerful and erotic. Your partner will make eyes! But you'll also get along great with brand new admirers. Keep the days around the first Advent weekend free for love!

♈ **Success** Work is fun, the money is right, and you are bursting with health. Only in the last days of December a familiar ghost visits you again in the form of existential worries, self-doubt, nervousness, bad mood. Thanks to Saturn in your zodiac sign, you know how to drive away the evil spirit: Pay no attention!

👍 **Good for** A great month with lots of love, fun and pleasure.

☹ **Bad for** Pessimism

✦ **Best star partners** Virgo, Gemini

Energy level Pisces: December 2024

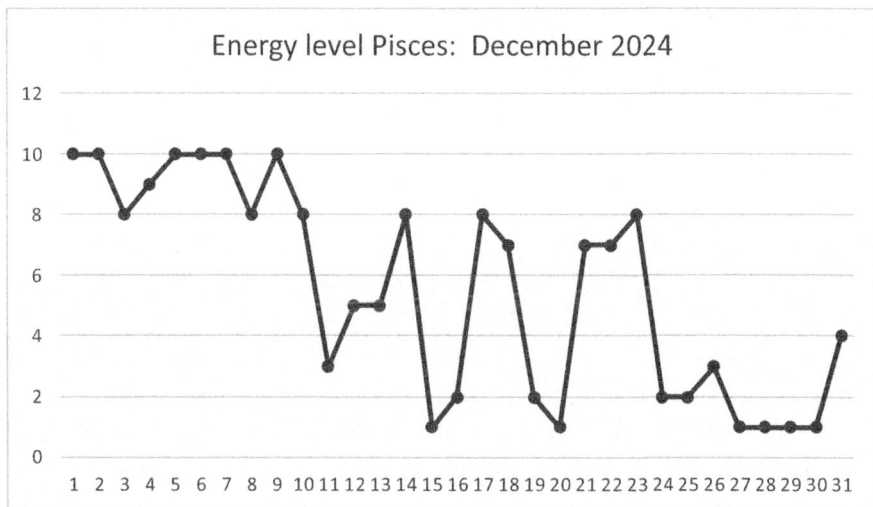

ARIES
(March 21-April 20)

You have a new friend in the sky. His name is Pluto. For 15 years he has not acknowledged you, often enough even hindered you. But in 2024 he finally acknowledges your strength. In this respect you have a splendid year ahead of you. This Pluto is not your only ally. After all, the year is ruled by the Sun. This benefits all twelve signs of the zodiac. This un wants you to do what you can, what suits you. These are wonderful prospects for you, an Aries who likes to do what he likes. Then, in the second half of the year, you also get lucky planet Jupiter in a fabulous position. If you are particularly lucky, you will win money. But you will certainly also be satisfied if you earn more, close a good deal, or succeed with an idea you have been carrying around for a long time. Then, of course, your personal ruler planet Mars will support you throughout the year. When exactly this will always be the case, please refer to the following monthly analysis. What you should pay attention to is Saturn. This planet is something like your personal watchdog. He always reports when you make mistakes and often before it even comes so far. So he is important. Now, in 2024, this planet is holding back. That is of course on the one hand very pleasant, because nobody reproaches you. But there it can happen that you notice too late when you are wrong. Now you have to take good care of yourself.

LOVE

Is a basic need for you, one can almost say it is as important as food and drink. You don't starve immediately if you lack it, but you starve in another way, namely that you lack joy of life and satisfaction. What does this look like for you in the coming year? As I said, the sun rules the new year. This means from the outset that you will certainly not suffer from a lack of love. In addition, there is Pluto, which causes something like a rejuvenation. Your body comes alive, you have more desire, and sexual satisfaction is an absolute highlight for you. Jupiter makes you the happiest. As mentioned earlier, starting in June this planet takes a position

in the sky that helps you In Love Again Our Mayl boy we get so many of these here Vista Yes yes yes do you say okay please a warning that my my full week I've already kicked out a few dogs already again full what I understand to be. Especially if you live alone, have no partners, you can almost take a bet on that changing in the second half of 2024. Something emanates from you that really attracts the opposite sex. Of course, you can't hide either. This is quite important that you are sure from inside that you are a lovable and desirable person.

Starlight leads, successes come,
love awakens.

CAREER

Four forces in the sky are responsible for making you successful. Let's start with the Sun. It, as well as all other zodiac signs, will encourage you and always push you where there is something to get. Pluto, which, as we said, is one hundred percent on your side in 2024, motivates you, literally programs you, to do more and, above all, the right thing in life. This also includes a portion of ambition, because you need it if you want to get further up and earn more. Jupiter intervenes in your life only from June on, but then with all its power. He promises you success in summer and at the latest in autumn. Saturn is usually the fourth force, to success. But it has already been said, he is not on your side in 2024. You are not a person who thinks long and hard when you see an opportunity. You are a go-getter. That's wonderful and lets you pass everyone else who hesitates. But in 2024, the danger is that you will be too quick and make mistakes. You just have to know that and keep reminding yourself to take care of yourself.

CHARACTER:	Bold, optimistic, elemental
PERSONAL APPEARANCE:	Energetic, powerful, brash
FEELING: Hot, passionate	
STONE:	Ruby
ANIMAL:	Wolf
POWER:	Thistle
BEST DAY:	Tuesday

24

JANUARY

💜 **Love** Your prospects for love are brighter, as Venus is in a favorable position during the first three weeks of the month. However, since planet Mars is in Capricorn, as mentioned earlier, you should not expect physical experiences to come easily to you. Now it's about confirming love not only in bed.

🏆 **Success** You will also benefit from Mars in January. He is in Capricorn, a sure sign that successes don't just fall from the sky, but have to be worked hard for. In other words, it depends on you now. A particularly promising week is right oh after the new moon on January 11.

👍 **Good for** Advance in love

☹ **Bad for** Wanting to achieve something with all your might

✦ **Best star partners** Sagittarius, Libra, Leo

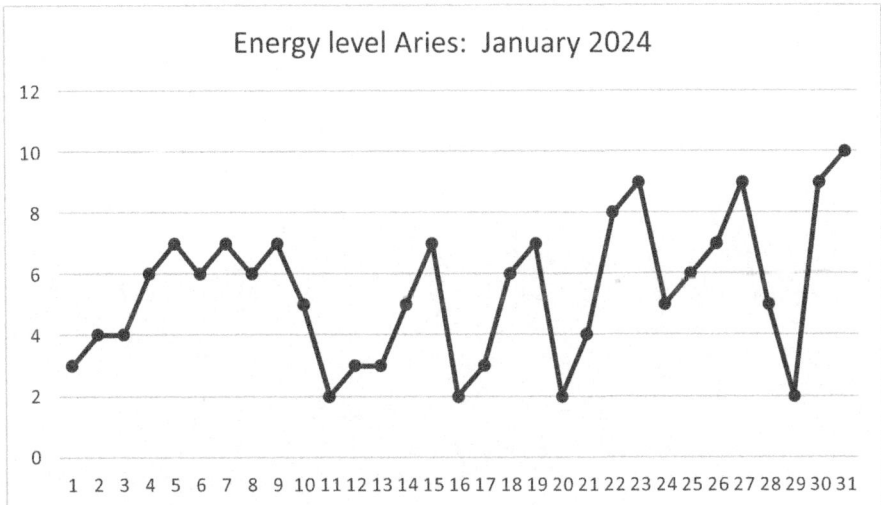

Energy level Aries: January 2024

FEBRUARY

♥ *Love* Mars and Venus move through Capricorn by mid-month. Take it as a sign to get busy with your partnership. What counts now is the willingness to adjust to each other, to accept the other as he is. Then, whether the 15th, the love duo lingers in Aquarius. This reveals an exciting love life.

♕ *Success* Pluto and Mercury in the sign of Aquarius could be an occasion to change one or the other thing that annoys you professionally. But be cautious. Saturn in the sign Pisces makes you not pay careful enough attention to unpleasant things. This also relates to how you handle your money. Jupiter in Taurus makes you generous, but sometimes also wasteful.

👍 *Good for* Professional advance after the 20th of the month

☹ *Bad for* Rash action

✦ *Best star partners* Aquarius, Leo

Energy level Aries: February 2024

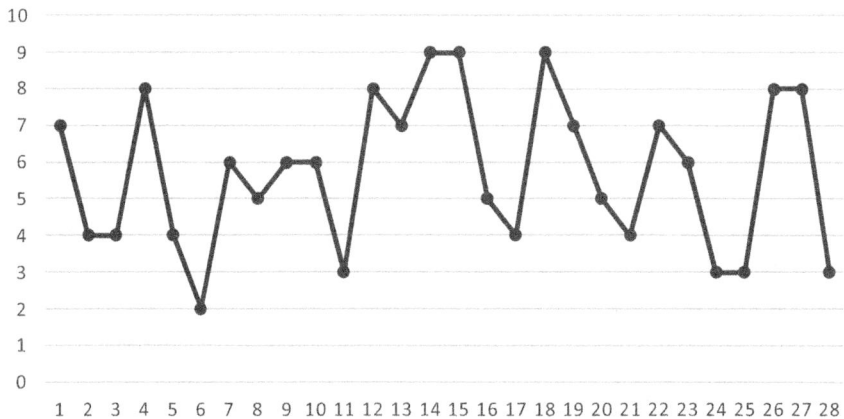

MARCH

💜 **Love** Until March 10, the love planet Venus reMayns in the zodiac sign Aquarius and thus in a favorable relationship with your sign. Mars stays even longer, until the 22nd. In this respect, it is quite possible that you will experience beautiful things in love in March. Unfortunately, this does not last until the beginning of spring on the 20th. Mars and Venus are already in the zodiac sign Pisces. There you can only dream of love. .

🏆 **Success** In terms of career the stars are unfavorable. Uranus and Jupiter exert pressure on your zodiac sign. So prepare yourself for a rather average month. When the Sun enters your zodiac sign Aries on the 20th, things will definitely get better.

👍 **Good for** You need patience

☹ **Bad for** Wanting to achieve something with all your might

✦ **Best star partners** Aries, Libra, Gemini

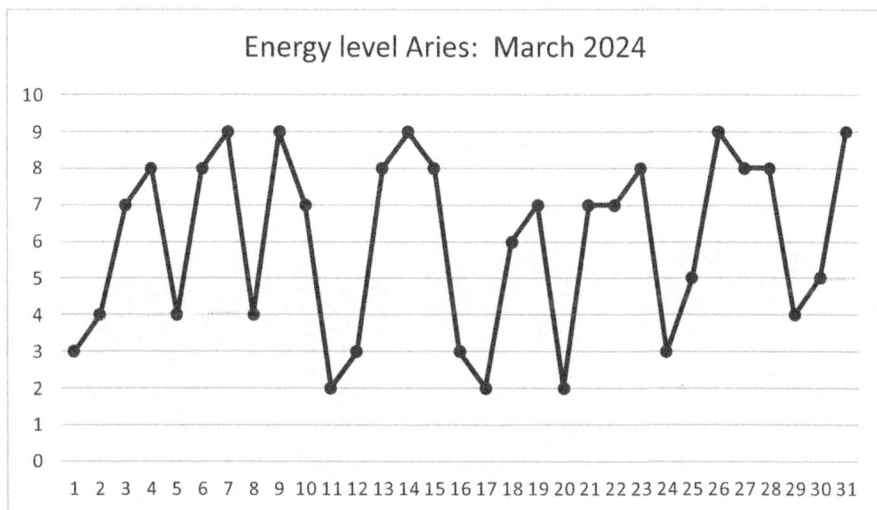

Energy level Aries: March 2024

APRIL

💜 **Love** You are one of the lucky ones: In addition to the Sun, Venus, the love planet, is at your side in the first half of the month. This awakens strength of heart that makes everything possible.

🏆 **Success** Take care of the important matters right in the first three weeks. Then the Sun, Mercury and Venus provide you with the luck you need to be successful. You yourself will be amazed at how well everything goes, how much self-confidence you have, how clear (and fast) your decisions turn out. Maybe the stars will throw you in at the deep end or be particularly tough. But with your life experience you are up to such challenges.

👍 **Good for** Simply being happy

☹ **Bad for** Doubting yourself and life

✦ **Best star partners** Aries, Libra, Aquarius Gemini

Energy level Aries: April 2024

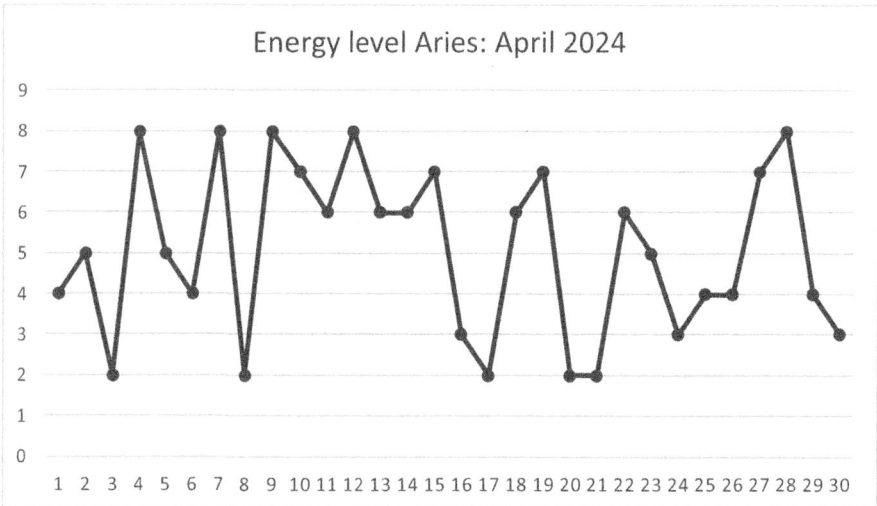

28

MAY

💜 **Love** You are lucky. With it the interhuman is meant. Everything speaks for the fact that the singles among you finally meet their soul partner. An invigorating, fresh breeze arises in relationships, which is a lot of fun for both of you. From the 20th on, it gets even more fantastic, because now you have Mars and Venus on your side. Assume that they will stage wonderful love scenes for you.

🏆 **Success** Mars is in your zodiac sign. On the one hand, you are grateful that you can get more energy via this planet, make better decisions, and also push forward when necessary. But this Mars has the big disadvantage that you easily become impatient. You need to know this and consciously hold back in some circumstances.

👍 **Good for** anything that needs strength

☹ **Bad for** impatience

✦ **Best star partners** Leo, Aries, Libra, Aquarius

Energy level Aries: May 2024

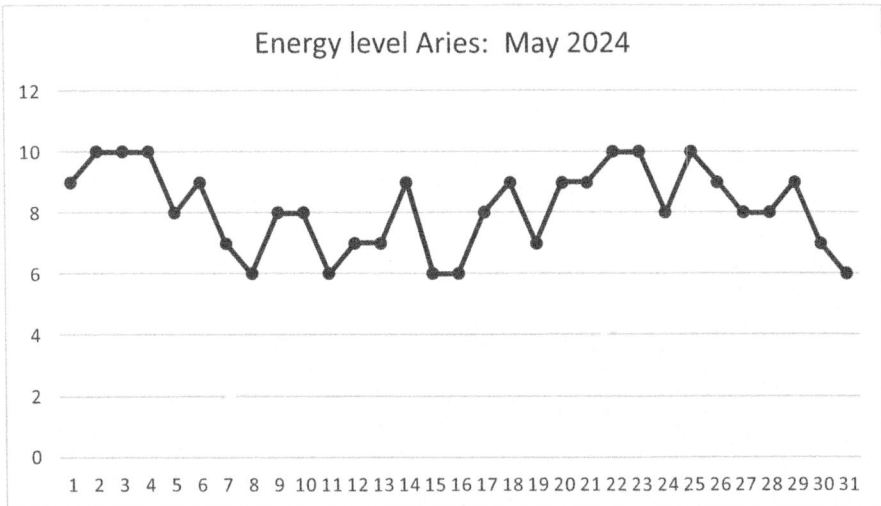

JUNE

💜 **Love** The locomotive of the year, the Sun, connects with Venus. That is super. With it miracles are possible. This helps you in love. There are no better conditions to experience a happy month with your sweetheart. Your chances are almost even better if you are looking for a partner. Especially if the Sun and Venus move very close together right in the first week, you will be very desirable and extremely desirable.

🏆 **Success** Lucky planet Jupiter takes a fabulous position in the first half of July. It can be concluded that you will be able to earn more money. Besides Jupiter, Venus also supports you, She arouses a kind of magnetism for money. And on June 4 Mercury takes an optimal position for business ventures.

👍 **Good for** Business, where something looks out for you

☹ **Bad for** leakage

✦ **Best star partners** Gemini, Libra

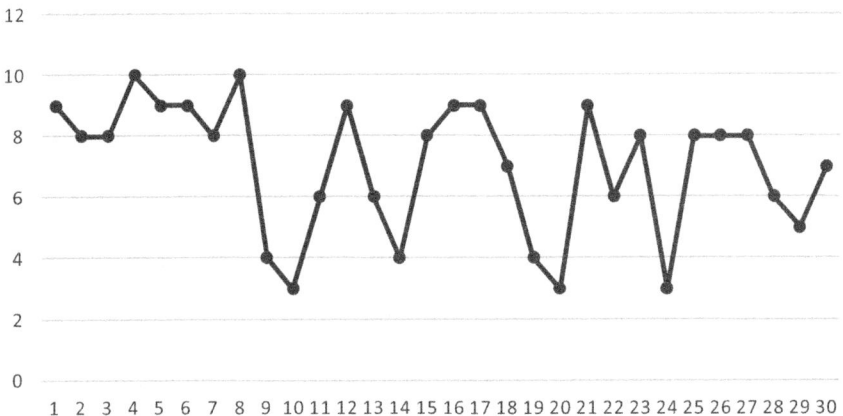

Energy level Aries: June 2024

JULY

♥ *Love* As far as love is concerned, you may not get what you want from your partner. But complain to the stars about it? Out of the question! You prove that you have profile and are up to the ups and downs of life. And at the end of the month it will be much better anyway with climax from full moon, July 21. There even a hot encounter is announced.

🏆 *Success* You are a routinier, a person who masters his life even without great cosmic support. Now, in July, this helps you well. To get through the days. In the last week you get the sun at your side. There you make very specific points.

👍 *Good for* staying positive

☹ *Bad for* Letting go

✦ *Best star partners* Leo

Energy level Aries: July 2024

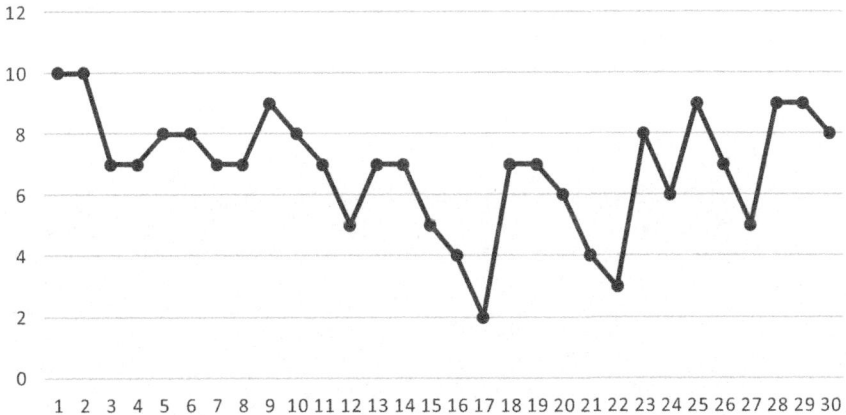

31

AUGUST

❤️ **Love** For you, it's summer throughout the month. Singles as well as couples experience a carefree time. You are happy not only on vacation. Honeymoon mood also spreads at home. Even after many years of marriage.

🏆 **Success** The sun rules the new year. Now, in August, it is in the sign of Leo. This is a fire sign, just like yours, Aries. This means you have a special connection with her and will be her favorite. This is a free ride into happiness. Problems will still arise sometimes. But you are never at a loss for a way out.

👍 **Good for** going out and meeting people

☹️ **Bad for** meaningy moods

✨ **Best star partners** Aquarius, Gemini

Energy level Aries: August 2024

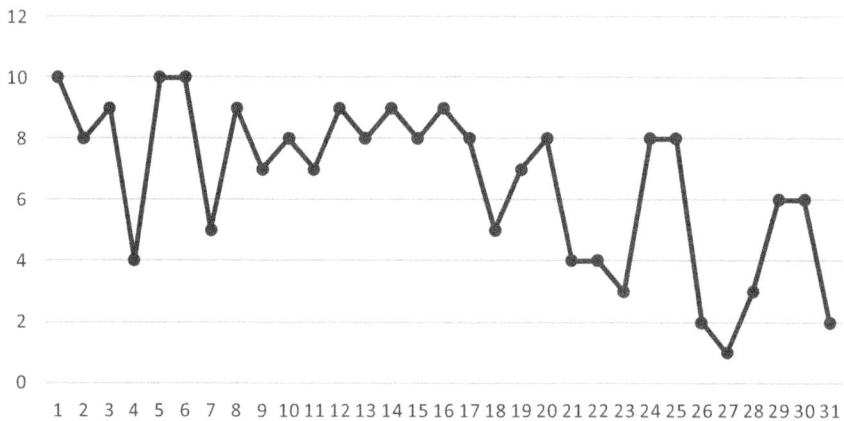

SEPTEMBER

💜 **Love** On September 6, your personal ruling planet Mars moves into the zodiac sign Cancer. If you are of the appropriate age, this will make you think not only of marriage, but even of starting a family. Those of you who are single will fully enjoy Venus. She's opposite your zodiac sign and makes sure that you'll catch on with potential partners - provided you also show that you're interested.

🏆 **Success** The Sun, regent of the year, is in Virgo in September. This supports your professional activities. Especially if you yourself believe more that you are good, it actually works out and you have more success.

👍 **Good for** family formation

☹ **Bad for** staying alone

✦ **Best star partners** Gemini, Aquarius

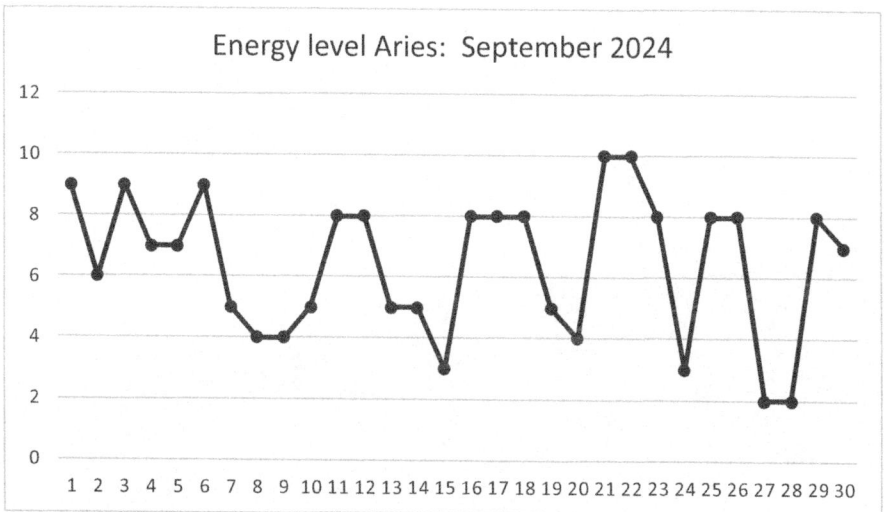

Energy level Aries: September 2024

OCTOBER

❤️ **Love** This is quite annoying. The sun is exactly opposite your zodiac sign in Libra. Normally, you can infer a magical month of love from this. But Mars and Venus are hiding in the sky, making your prospects in love drop to zero.

🏆 **Success** Planet Jupiter is helping you and clearing difficulties out of your way. If you get stopped anyway, it's only to show how good you really are. Another important note: in October, the fine print is also especially important. This means you should be very precise and expect surprises.

👍 **Good for** optimism even when things don't go so well

☹️ **Bad for** letting yourself go

✦ **Best star partners** Gemini

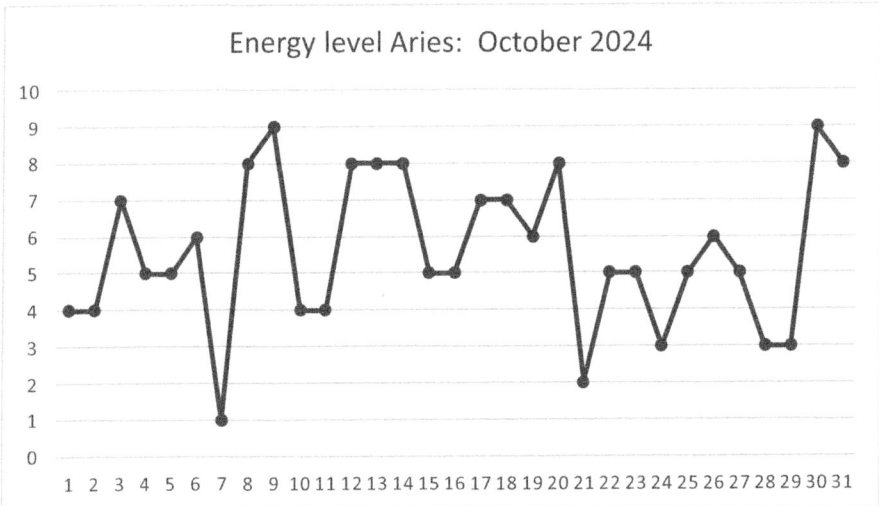

Energy level Aries: October 2024

NOVEMBER

💜 **Love** At the beginning of the month you have again the chance for the big drama; unless you realize in time how much you exaggerate. The second half of November strengthens your partnership. But this also requires that you are open for each other.

🏆 **Success** During the first two weeks of November it's called: Please wait! The smooth flow of business of any kind is disturbed. Resolutions with hand and foot are scarce. Appointments are often not kept. Agreements are not worth much. Best, you postpone important matters to the second month

👍 **Good for** Don't let yourself be pulled down

☹ **Bad for** self-doubt

✦ **Best star partners** Leo

Energy level Aries: November 2024

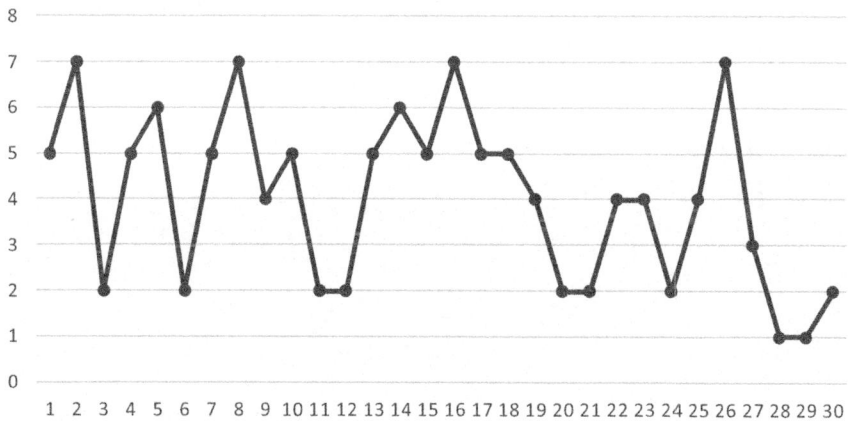

DECEMBER

♥ **Love** In December, you wake up in the morning with a smile, and wherever you are drawn during the day - to the hustle and bustle or to solitude - you have cozy, pleasurable and soulful experiences. The stars rumor of an encounter: A person with whom you get along very well from the head, convinces also with sex.

🏆 **Success** And the whole December has promising days for your career. It will be really exciting; the stars attest to your fabulous negotiating skills. People will buy everything from you. So that you should not think about your career at Christmas, the stars retreat now.

👍 **Good for** being happy

☹ **Bad for** doubting yourself

✦ **Best star partners** Gemini, Aries, Libra

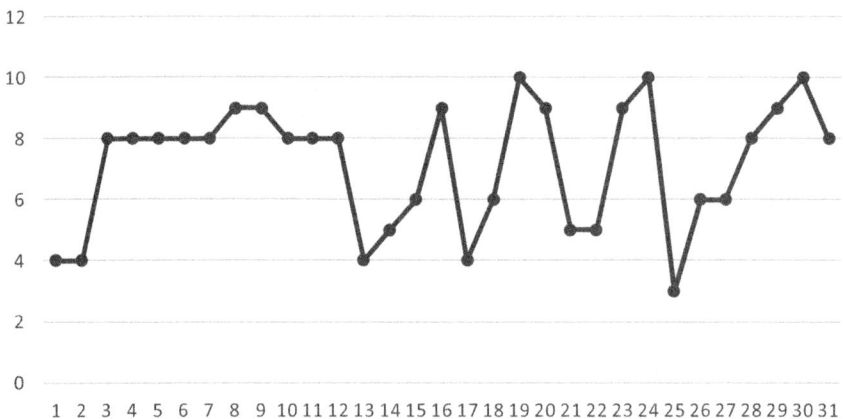

Energy level Aries: December 2024

TAURUS
(April 21-May 21)

Every year, a different cosmic quantity determines the race on Earth. In 2024, it is the sun. It rules the year. For a bull this brings advantages. Your strengths and abilities can come into full play. You will be successful and happy and earn more money. Now the thing is, your successes don't just fall from the sky either. There are conditions. The stipulations come from the planet Pluto, which is in the zodiac sign Aquarius for most of the year. This is a difficult position for you. It demands flexibility from you. Situations will arise again and again in the coming year in which you will not be able to cope with any routine measures. "I've always done it this way. Why shouldn't it be that way now ...?" This sentence loses usefulness and usefulness. "Aha, it looks like I have to do things differently,..." This sentence, on the other hand, is used more and more often. So it all depends on how flexible you are and whether you are ready for change. If so, you have a good year ahead of you. Accordingly, it will be difficult if you stick to the way you have always done. Pronounced favorable is Jupiter. He bears the name lucky planet and is in your zodiac sign in the first half of the year. Now you can make up your own mind what this means for you. What is certain is that you will not suffer from money problems at all. On the contrary, you will get more. In the second half of the year this Jupiter moves into the sign Gemini. Then again more flexibility is required. Saturn is also very important. This star is your overseer. He takes care that you don't make any mistakes and if you do, you correct them immediately. In 2024 he takes a break. That means you have to get along without him, which in turn means you have to be careful and conscientious. Then, of course, your personal ruling planet, Venus, is also important. It moves through all twelve signs of the zodiac, as it does every year, sometimes strong, other times rather weak. How this affects you in detail, you will find out in the monthly analyses.

LOVE

Your great stars make it possible that you are not only loved but also understood in 2024 and sometimes feel like a baked fish who is happily in love for the first time. Unless your current partner has a very messed up horoscope, you will definitely move closer together again and taste that wonderful feeling of not being alone in this world. An important influence here also comes from Pluto and Uranus. It will be worth your while if you tune in to them from the very beginning: These stars don't like compromise. You may be lucky and already have a life with someone who meets this standard. If you live alone and are looking for a partner, you'll be fine in 2024, because the effect of these two planets is decidedly favorable. You can almost say the whole world is looking for a partner in 2024, whether you live alone or not. Accordingly, it is easy to start a relationship.

"Sun shines, success follows.
Taurus: Happy and strong."

CAREER

Uranus and Pluto ensure that your life becomes more interesting, varied and exciting. You may move to another city, start a new job, meet interesting people, or perhaps even prevail in a competition and become well-known. Then there's Jupiter, the lucky planet, to mention right away. He hacks into your zodiac sign in the first half of the year and will take you to where luck is waiting for you. Don't just think of material luck here. That is also associated with this star, but even more so it is a happiness that grows from within and takes hold of your whole person. The fact that Saturn does not really fulfill his task as a watchdog has already been said, also that you have to take over his function. Basically, it can be said that the second half of the year is better than the first, both financially and career-wise.

CHARACTER:	Fun-loving, helpful, comfortable
PERSONAL APPEARANCE:	Modest, determined, tolerant
FEELING:	Natural, affectionate
STONE:	Emerald
ANIMAL:	Maybug
POWER:	Pumpkin
BEST DAY:	Friday

JANUARY

💜 *Love* The love planet Venus is in the sign of Sagittarius. There the strange and new appeals: Therefore high season for all single bulls among you. But of course this time also benefits those who are already in a committed relationship: Maybe they have to come up with something new.

🏆 *Success* Jupiter helps and Mars stands by him. Together with the Sun and Mercury, they form a quartet that opens up great opportunities for you. Uranus brings joy. However, what it brings is not necessarily what you already know. But if you get involved, you'll have a wonderful time

👍 *Good for* Taking time for love

☹ *Bad for* Getting bogged down with trivialities.

✦ *Best star partners* Pisces, Cancer, Scorpio

Energy level Taurus: January 2024

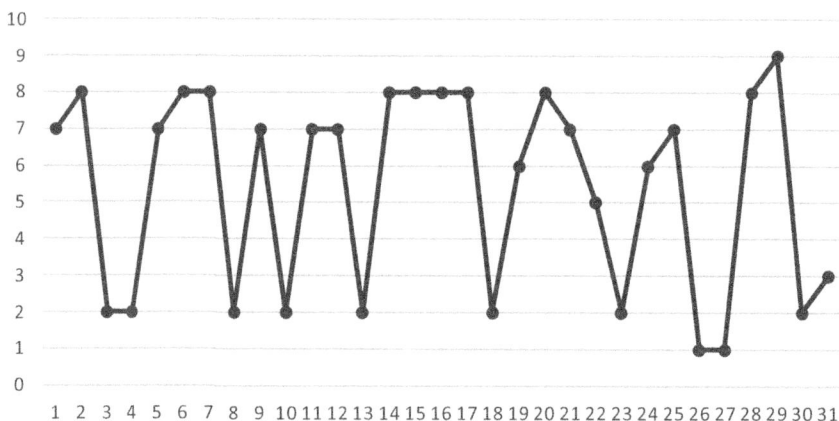

FEBRUARY

Now Pluto is in the zodiac sign Aquarius, where it will stay for over 15 years. So it is definitely not wrong to get ready for it now: Pluto demands change. It means letting go of habits to make way for something new and better.

♥ *Love* Until the middle of February, Mars and Venus, the love duo, will take care of you. This fits in well with Carnival, which is on at the same time. There one must advise you almost not to exaggerate. During the carnival, namely, new relationships arise quickly.

♈ *Success* Until the 20th of the month, the Sun is in the zodiac sign Aquarius. This requires flexibility. You must not be too narrow-minded now. Then, in the last ten days, the Sun and Saturn are all on your side. There is also one or the other unexpected success possible.

👍 *Good for* following your inner destiny

☹ *Bad for* quarrels and arguments

✦ *Best star partners* Pisces, Taurus, Virgo

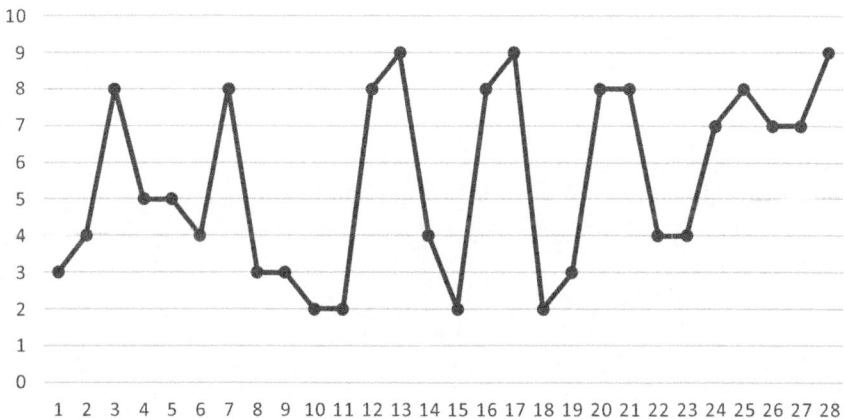

Energy level Taurus: February 2024

MARCH

💜 **Love** On March 11, love planet Venus moves into a favorable position to your zodiac sign. This already tastes a bit like spring. If you wait a few more days now, it will be even better because Mars will also take a favorable position to your zodiac sign then. Spring begins on March 20. A love miracle is possible for you now.

🏆 **Success** The Sun makes you sleepy. However, you must not give in to this feeling, because Jupiter and Uranus are in your zodiac sign Taurus and demand success. Nothing helps, you must overcome yourself and do what is possible.

👍 **Good for** Promising

☹ **Bad for** Worrying

✦ **Best star partners** Taurus, Virgo, Capricorn

Energy level Taurus: March 2024

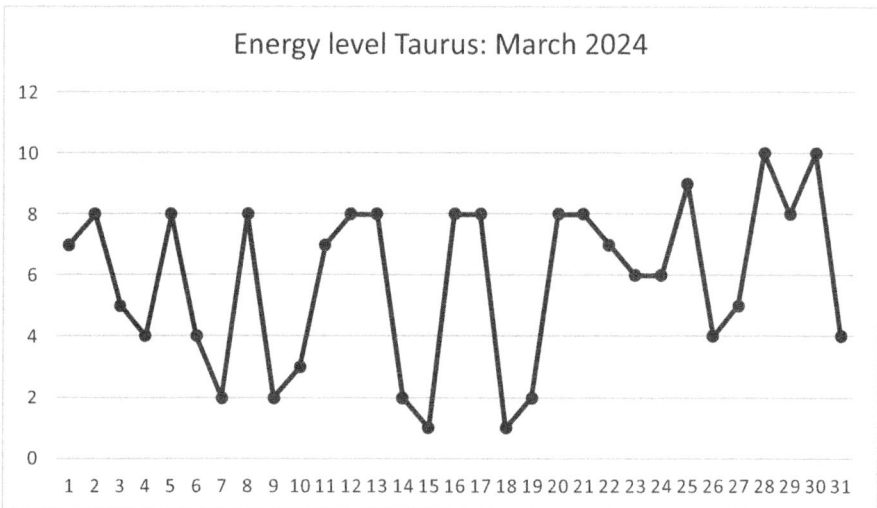

APRIL

💜 **Love** Love is beautiful, but dissonance also occurs. The reason: Mars and Venus pass through different signs, so they do not complement each other. But there is nothing in the stars about unhappiness. Maybe you should think of something to surprise your partner with, even if it's just a nice spring bouquet.

🏆 **Success** Uranus and Jupiter come closer and closer in April. It's like you have an antenna right up in the sky. Everything you wish for arrives above, is tested, and may come true. On the 20th, the Sun also enters your zodiac sign Taurus: now miracles are possible.

👍 **Good for** fostering friendships

☹ **Bad for** discouragement

✦ **Best star partners** Cancer, Pisces, Scorpio

Energy level Taurus: April 2024

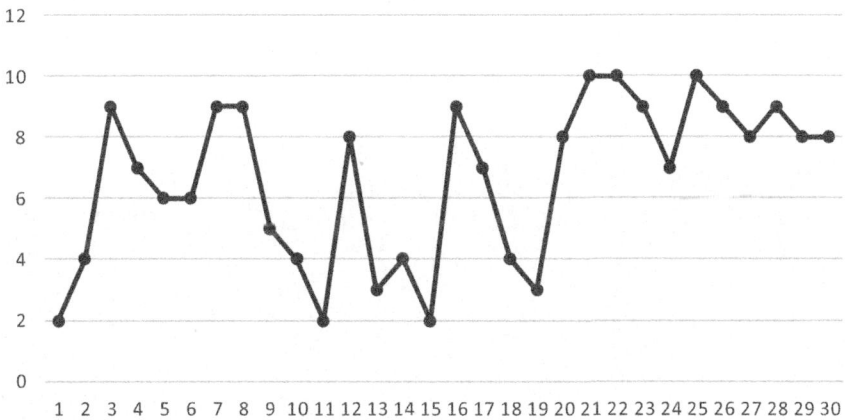

MAY

💜 **Love** Venus moves through your star sign. This gives you charisma. You stand out, you arrive, you are admired. Unfortunately Mars is running behind this Venus again like last month. This could also happen to you and it will not come to the happy finale. Only in the last week of May it could work out.

🏆 **Success** Sun, Mercury, Venus, Uranus and Jupiter manage your career path until the 20th: You owe this cosmic team perseverance, tenacity and resourcefulness, so that you never capitulate before obstacles. They also network you with the right (and important) people and make you unbeatable in negotiations

👍 **Good for** Forging your life's work

☹ **Bad for** Dwelling on trifles

✦ **Best star partners** Scorpio, Pisces, Taurus

Energy level Taurus: May 2024

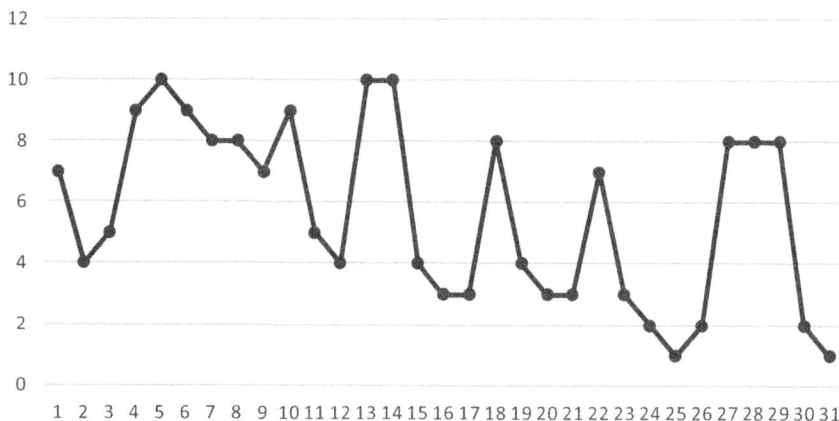

44

JUNE

💜 **Love** Mars is in an unfavorable position to your zodiac sign during the first week of June. But then you make up for everything you missed during the first week: Now Mars is in your zodiac sign. Things get even better on the 17th, where planet Venus enters into a relationship with him. You will experience a wonderful time.

🏆 **Success** Uranus is in your zodiac sign and is strengthened by Saturn. As a result, its effect is better than usual. Is there a threat of danger? No, never, if you are open and ready for change. Now, for God's sake, don't hold on to everything that has always been the way it is. Be ready for new things, you will be happy. If something important is coming up, put it on the second half of the month if possible.

👍 **Good for** Significantly more self-confidence

🙁 **Bad for** holding yourself back

✦ **Best star partners** Cancer, Pisces, Scorpio

Energy level Taurus: June 2024

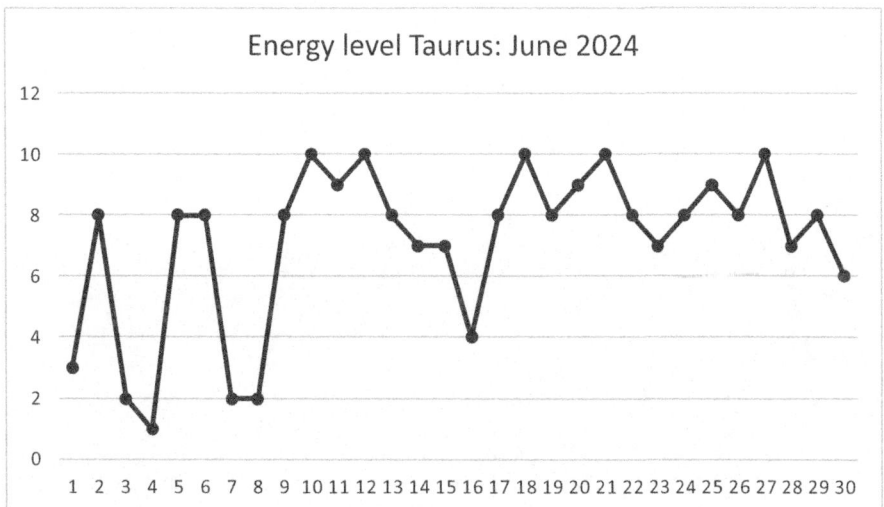

JULY

💜 **Love** By the 12th of the month, Venus moves into a favorable position to your zodiac sign. This will have a very favorable effect on your love life. Don't expect heaven on earth right away, but you will have more luck than usual. After the middle of the month, there could also be a dimming of your love prospects. Bear it with dignity if you don't feel as much love as usual.

🏆 **Success** Until the 18th Mars provides you with energy. But then you won't get any more power from the heavens, so you'll have to take care of it yourself. How do you do that? Live healthy and do sports. In your diet, make sure you get the right minerals and vitamins. You can get information at any drugstore or pharmacy.

👍 **Good for** inner and outer growth

☹ **Bad for** fake for commitment, pretend

✦ **Best star partners** Capricorn, Cancer, Virgo

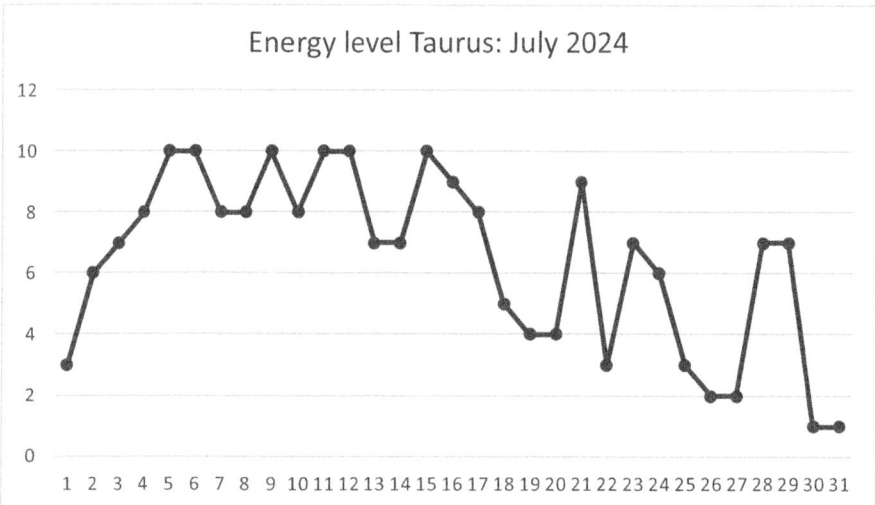

Energy level Taurus: July 2024

AUGUST

♥ **Love** The love planet Venus holds its hand protectively over you throughout the month. This provides happiness hormones with everything that is fun. Sometimes this can be chocolate, a live concert or a night dancing the night away. Some also find a special kick in sports.

♈ **Success** A travel tip at this point: Visit places that are completely new to you. With Uranus in your luggage, this will be much more exciting than a trip as a repeat offender. In addition, you feel deep happiness in the circle of dear friends, because you feel accepted, respected and secure. Therefore, nurture your friendships like a marriage.

👍 **Good for** self-affirmation

☹ **Bad for** getting dragged down

✦ **Best star partners** Cancer, Virgo, Capricorn

Energy level Taurus: August 2024

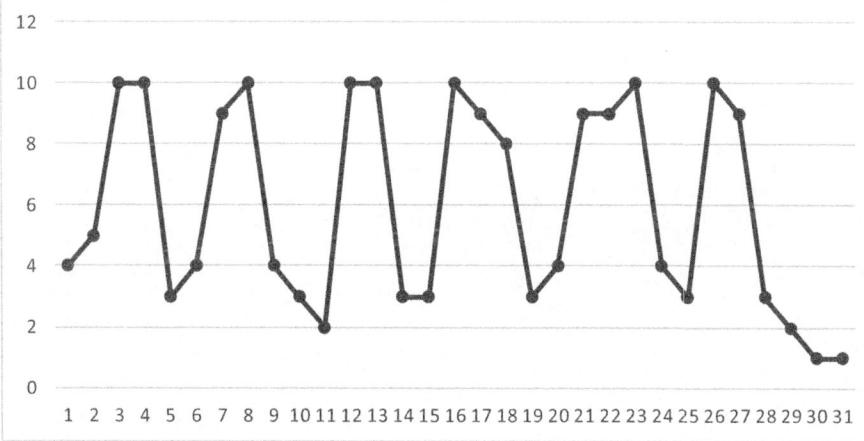

SEPTEMBER

♥ **Love** Your love life can develop fully thanks to Mars in friendly sextile to your zodiac sign. You meet your partner anew, without expectations, without resenting him, just glad he exists. The Sun as regent of the new year in trine to your zodiac sign gives you more courage and self-confidence.

♕ **Success** The Sun in Virgo and Mars in the zodiac sign Cancer give self-confidence and even awaken the desire to take responsibility. You are already successful? Bravo, but you can do even better. You get more leeway and are allowed to take responsibility for projects yourself. The sun makes you courageous. So courageous that you demand more money and recognition.

👍 **Good for** brainstorming

☹ **Bad for** letting yourself go

✦ **Best star partners** Capricorn, Scorpio

Energy level Taurus: September 2024

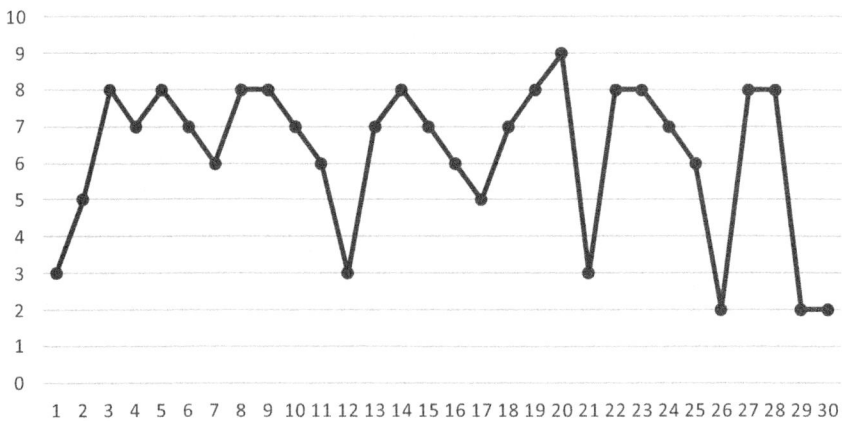

OCTOBER

💜 **Love** The planets Mars and Venus hook under each other. This has a magical effect on your love life: Your sex awakens, new partners enter your life, your relationships sizzle. Very special fortune is granted to couples who are now walking down the aisle to get married.

🏆 **Success** The stars for your professional life are less friendly. Many career traffic lights are on yellow, signaling that a cautious and careful approach is right. You absolutely need phases for recovery again and again, so that you function one hundred percent. Right at the beginning of the month the new moon hole sucks on your strength: Take it easy! Then, from the 18th, the lights turn green, and by the end of the month you are up to any challenge.

👍 **Good for** climax

☹ **Bad for** self-doubt

✦ **Best star partners** Capricorn, Virgo, Taurus

Energy level Taurus: October 2024

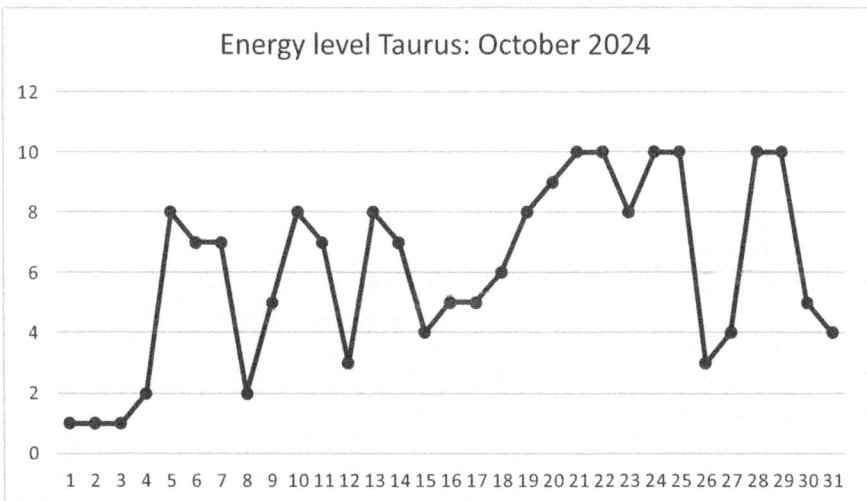

NOVEMBER

💜 **Love** By the 10th of the month, your prospects are bright. You have the green light. You may even catch the great love. In any case, you enjoy closeness and intimacy. However, this requires that you are not too casual with your feelings and those of your partner. The Sun is now in the zodiac sign of Scorpio and demands depth and devotion.

🏆 **Success** You can also count on the fulfillment of professional hopes. The energy dip around the New Moon on November 1 is particularly strong this time. On the last ten days of November, everyone just seems to want something from you. Always take a deep breath - and don't go crazy!

👍 **Good for** Intense living

☹ **Bad for** Withdrawal

✦ **Best star partners** Capricorn, Cancer

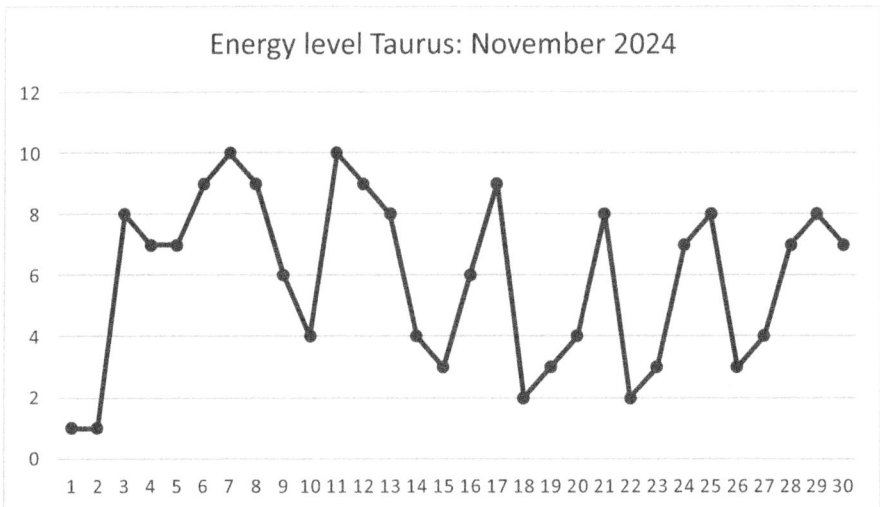

Energy level Taurus: November 2024

DECEMBER

♥ **Love** As far as love is concerned, the stars are extremely frugal. Venus, the love planet, doesn't spring into action. But an epicure like you, knows how to make a lot out of a little. For example, you can surprise your partner with a particularly nice Christmas gift. How about a skiing tour or a trip to the south.

♕ **Success** You are in top form until after the middle of the month. This is especially beneficial at work: You react more quickly, are concentrated and have the right ideas at the right time. You are also on the spot when it comes to encouraging others, which makes you extremely popular with your colleagues and friends.

👍 **Good for** Allowing yourself something

☹ **Bad for** Self-discipline, being able to control yourself

✦ **Best star partners** Capricorn, Virgo

Energy level Taurus: December 2024

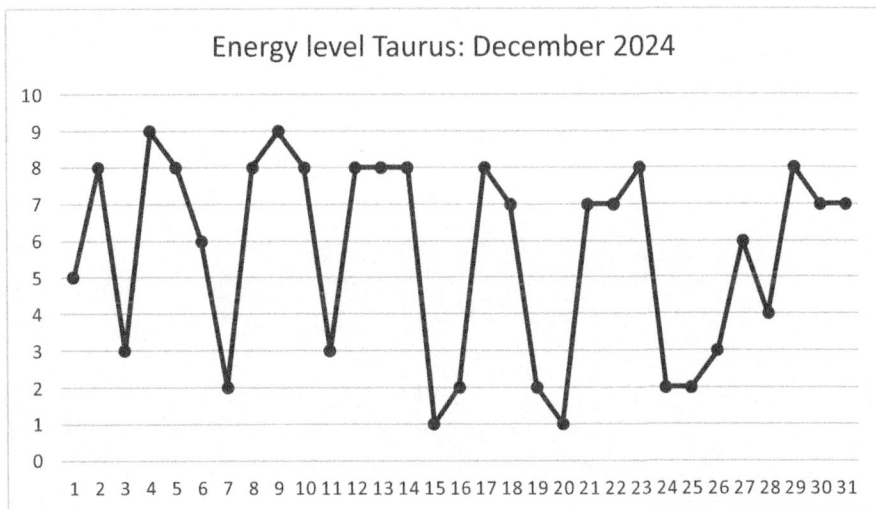

GEMINI
(May 22-June 21)

The sun determines how 2024 will be. It is the government for the year and awakens your best qualities: Knowledge, experience and kindness. That alone is enough for a successful year. But there are two more pluses: Pluto and Jupiter. One, Pluto, which has left you on the left for years, shows you its positive side in 2024. He is in a friendly trine to your zodiac sign and can thus fully assert his positive influences, namely that you have more to say. After all, as a Gemini you possess a very important task in life. You are supposed to make sure that the people of our world understand each other, live together and get along well. You may even be given a position of responsibility. But even if things just continue as before, you will have more to say than before. Perhaps you will also write for a newspaper and be able to contribute your opinion there. You also know quite instinctively that things cannot go on as before. The world must change, become friendlier and fairer. You will represent this concern in 2024. Another important planet is Uranus. He is in Taurus and thus in the sign next to you and thus also has a strong influence. What does he want? The answer is friendship and reconciliation. You will become closer with the people you know in 2024 and make many new friends. You will be especially happy about planet Jupiter. This star enters your zodiac sign on May 25. Now when you hear what its second name is, lucky planet, you KNOW what awaits you in 2024: great opportunities at work, more money, and a better quality of life. With Jupiter in your zodiac sign, you may also get a desire to change your life, take up a new profession or learn something you've always had in mind. Whatever it is, Jupiter will support you. Saturn is also important. He'll make sure you don't do anything stupid. Because as I said, you truly have great stars through Jupiter, the Sun and Uranus. There one could easily fall into the opinion now no borders would be set to you. Wrong, completely wrong! You need this Saturn to really improve your life.

LOVE

The Sun and Pluto strengthen your ability to love, make sure you give more space to relaxation, leisure and pleasure. You allow yourself more frequent evenings out, meeting friends, or dating your partner (old or new). Your hormones also experience a kind of springtime: sex is fun - and fun is yours to have. It's as simple as that. Singles benefit from this lust for life just as much as couples: you have more desire for and with each other. The second half of the year also promises wonderful times for love, because Jupiter is in your zodiac sign. Couples who have found each other this year will go down the aisle. And singles? Are no more - and are looking around for a shared apartment.

Stars shine, dreams live -.
Year of success 2024!

CAREER

The best news in advance: in 2024 you are satisfied with yourself. It's a feeling that comes from within. You feel good about yourself. You don't define happiness solely in terms of your job or your income. It is due to your radiance that people take notice of you. You are an enrichment for every company, because you carry qualities in you that are not found anywhere else: You are humorous, a team player, optimistic. This miracle mix lets you be even more successful than before. Whether you are an employee, entrepreneur or freelancer. Let me talk about Pluto again: this powerful star is in a friendly trine to your star sign. This means that you have all the positive achievements, abilities and powers of your ancestors. This makes you irrepressibly strong and experienced in life. However, you must be open to these powers. This means thinking respectfully of those who came before you.

CHARACTER:	Curious, lively, versatile
PERSONAL APPEARANCE:	Suave, charming, winning
FEELING:	Dualistic
STONE:	Carnelian
ANIMAL:	Fox
POWER:	Ivy
BEST DAY:	Wednesday

JANUARY

♥ **Love** Love primarily aligns with the course of the planet Venus for you. If it is in a favorable angle to your zodiac sign, as it is now in January, there will be more lust and joy in your life - and accordingly there will be more exciting dates for singles and more frolicking and making love in partnerships.

♈ **Success** January will be rather average. It is called duties to do, push service after regulation and not immediately revolt, if something runs against your head. You will reap the fruits of this sovereign behavior in January. At the end of the month the love stars are particularly generous to you: A surprise is in order.

👍 **Good for** calm and composure

☹ **Bad for** Actions no matter what

✦ **Best star partners** you yourself

Energy level Gemini: January 2024

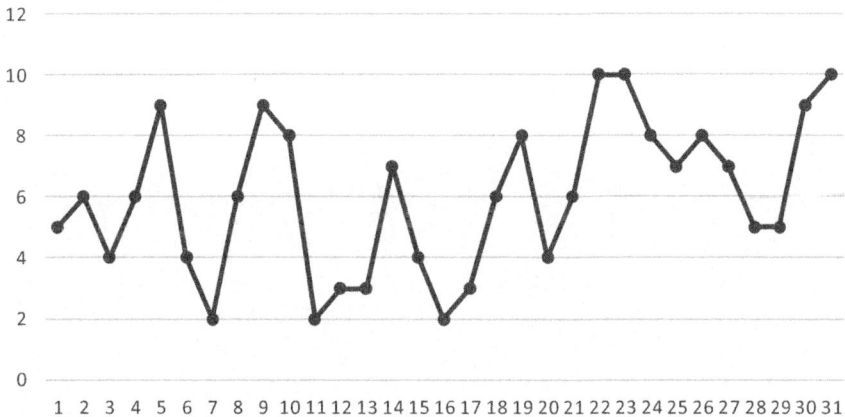

FEBRUARY

Now Pluto is in the zodiac sign Aquarius, where it will stay for almost 20 years. So it's certainly not wrong to get ready for it now: Pluto demands change. It means letting go of habits to make way for something new and better.

♥ *Love* The Sun and Mercury help you take life from the light side. Mars and Venus, however, stay in Capricorn until mid-month, a rather unfavorable position for you. Big love stories run, if at all, only after the carnival in the second half of the month.

♕ *Success* The month certainly gives you one or the other perk. But a big success is missing. Saturn blocks, and Jupiter is not on your side either. There you have to be satisfied if small things succeed.

👍 *Good for* People who stand firmly by your side

☹ *Bad for* Not taking responsibility for your life.

✦ *Best star partners* Aquarius, Gemini, Sagittarius

Energy level Gemini: February 2024

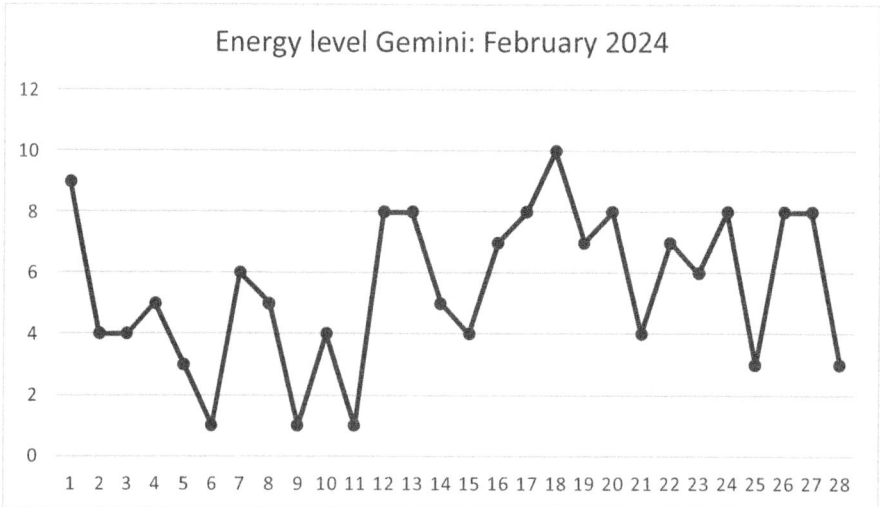

56

MARCH

💜 *Love* Until March 10, love plays the leading role in your life. Whether a hot affair will happen right away is uncertain, but you're sure to have a lot of fun with your partner. Unfortunately, you can't take your great love prospects over to spring. It starts on the 20th, but Mars and Venus, the planets that take care of love, are now far and wide nowhere to be seen.

🏆 *Success* Venus and Mars help you to good business, or advantageous negotiations with customers, colleagues and bosses. If then on 20. the sun officially heralds the spring, runs for you rather pure routine. In any case, there will be no major advantages.

👍 *Good for* Time for love

☹ *Bad for* Not being ready for change after March 6

✦ *Best star partners* Libra, Gemini, Sagittarius

Energy level Gemini: March 2024

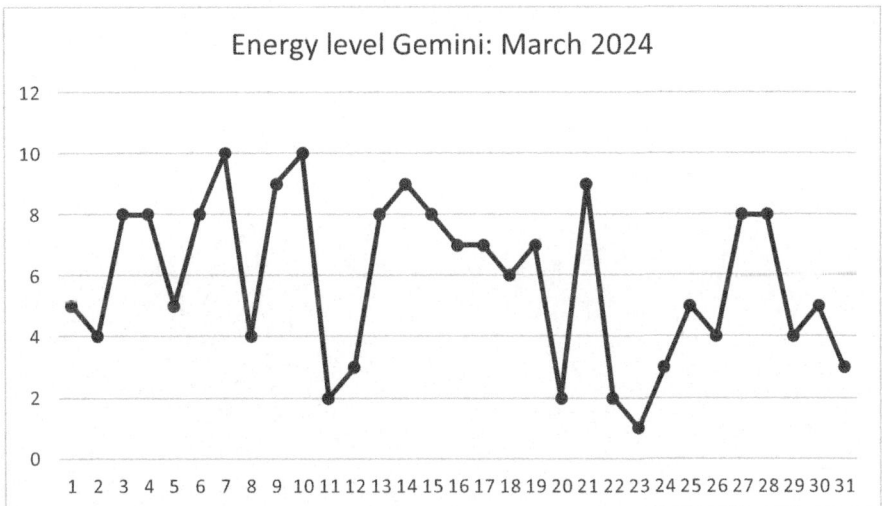

APRIL

💜 **Love** Mars in the zodiac sign of Pisces is heading for Neptune. For love, this means that it no longer matters what you look like or whether you have good sex, but whether you understand each other, and even more, complement each other. With these Neptune and Mars positions, it's no longer two people meeting, but two souls.

🏆 **Success** As long as the Sun is in the zodiac sign of Aries, that is, until the 20th, you'll do well at work. Mercury also conjoins Venus. As a result, everything you say comes across as believable.

👍 **Good for** Fulfillment in love

☹ **Bad for** Not taking time for the good things in life

✦ **Best star partners** Gemini, Sagittarius

Energy level Gemini: April 2024

MAY

♥ **Love** When Venus enters your zodiac sign in the last week of May, love blossoms. Everything points to a person coming into your life. You will fall in love with this being and he will fall in love with you. If you are single, you will have a wonderful time, and you will probably have found your life partner. If you are in a committed relationship, there are two possibilities. One is that you break out because you are convinced that you have found the better partner. The other is that you feel a more emotional love for the new person who has entered your life, but this will revitalize your existing two-way relationship.

♛ **Success** You should wait with all important matters until the end of the month, then the stars are clearly more favorable. Until that time comes, routine counts. You will nevertheless gain one or the other advantage.

👍 **Good for** Take it as it comes

☹ **Bad for** Don't waste your energy on projects that yield nothing.

✦ **Best star partners** Aquarius, Libra, Sagittarius

Energy level Gemini: May 2024

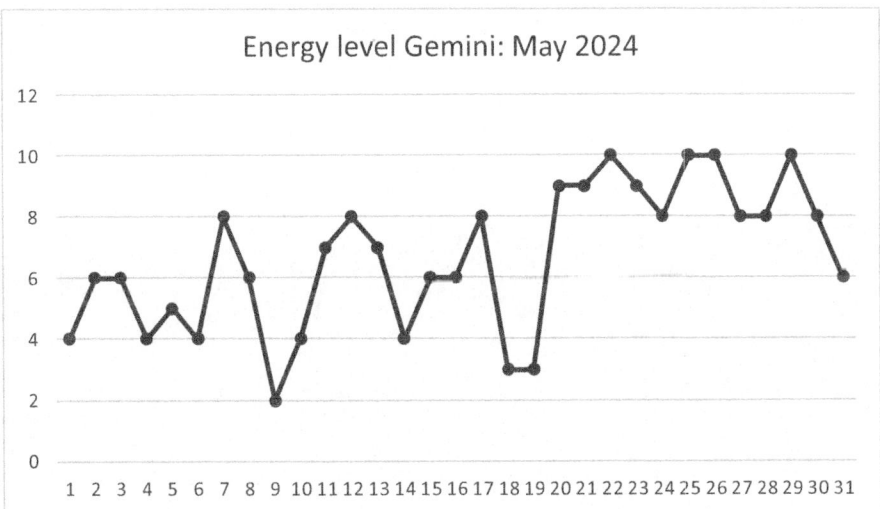

JUNE

♥ **Love** During the first week of June, planet Mars is in a favorable position to your zodiac sign. Some of you are likely to experience all-beautiful moments. Then Mars moves one sign further. Now you lack the right passion. It becomes even more unfavorable from the 17th of the month: Venus leaves you then.

♔ **Success** In the past, when money was paid at the end of the month of employment, this day was called "payday". Something very similar applies to you for al-most the entire month of June. The Sun, Venus and Jupiter are moving through your zodiac sign of Gemini. Things are on the upswing, perhaps even furiously so in some circumstances. Indulge yourself. Tell yourself once again that life is there to be enjoyed and to treat yourself.

👍 **Good for** acting wisely, stepping on the gas, love

☹ **Bad for** change, new initiatives, expanding your sphere of influence

✦ **Best star partners** Aquarius, Gemini, Sagittarius

Energy level Gemini: June 2024

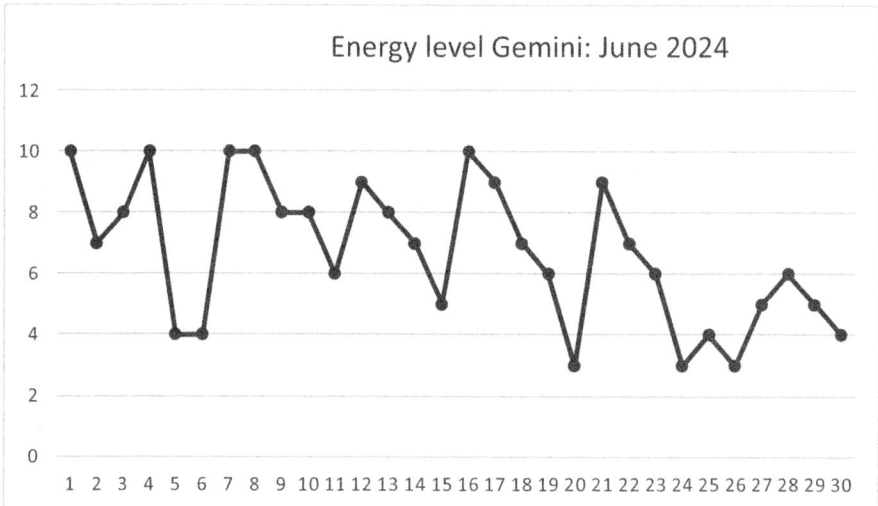

60

JULY

💜 *Love* Jupiter, the lucky planet, moves through your zodiac sign. Everywhere, privately and professionally, in love and money, you are therefore the zodiac sign that receives gifts. You may also be in love for the first time. If your current partner does not have a very difficult horoscope, you will definitely move closer together again and taste this wonderful feeling of not being alone in this world.

🏆 *Success* You sail under a favorable wind in July: Jupiter makes sure that you go through life with enviable nonchalance - and that although Saturn is in square to your zodiac sign. So it's not bad if you make friends with Saturn, acknowledge him, accept him. Then you can with him - and he with you. You know that you can accomplish something in life with Saturn.

👍 *Good for* Starting a relationship

☹ *Bad for* Getting stuckon problems

✦ *Best star partners* Aquarius, Gemini, Sagittarius

Energy level Gemini: July 2024

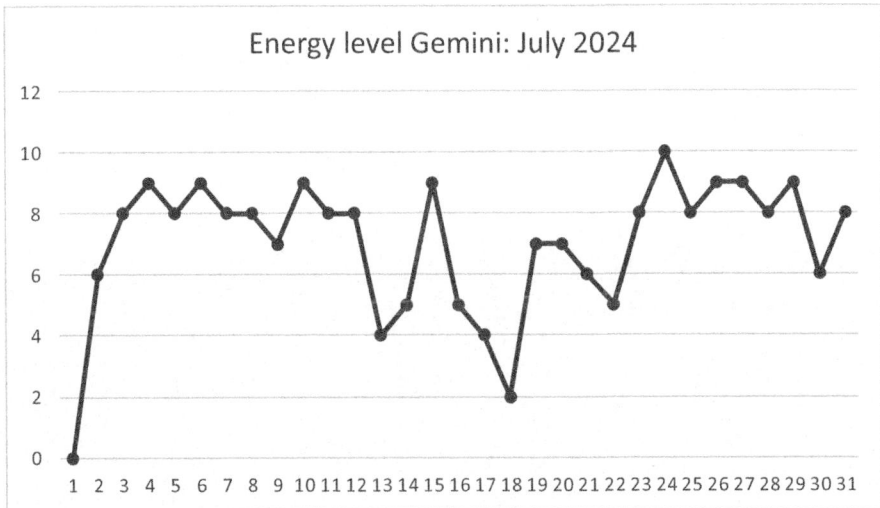

AUGUST

♥ *Love* The Sun as the regent of the new year brings enormous joie de vivre and even more sensuality. Mars awakens passion. Couples should take a little trip. An enchanting place makes happy. Singles have the best chances for promising encounters around the full moon on August 19.

🏆 *Success* Jupiter, the lucky planet, is in your zodiac sign and promotes your further development. Even Pluto gives his blessing: you will grow. Two paths lead to success: hard work and luck. The former you have to provide, luck is taken care of by the stars.

👍 *Good for* Showing your best side

☹ *Bad for* Giving yourself too little credit

✦ *Best star partners* Aquarius, Leo

Energy level Gemini: August 2024

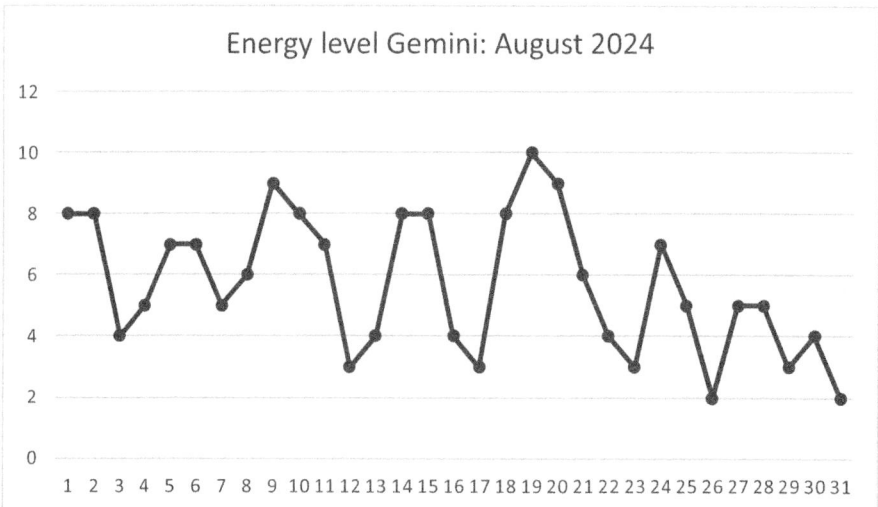

SEPTEMBER

💜 **Love** Jupiter is to blame. This planet sees is in your zodiac sign. There you have reason to be happy and experience more passion. Especially in bed. How this miracle comes about? You are incredibly romantic and inventive, like to play with your charms again and think about what might be fun and pleasing to your partner.

🏆 **Success** You need to learn to let yourself go even in your free time. A lazy weekend is not wasted, but a gain. Your body, and sometimes your psyche, need pit stops. Seek out places that give you peace of mind. Especially around the new moon on September 18, breaks are urgently needed. An autumn walk, for example, is golden.

👍 **Good for** Experience and enjoy love

☹ **Bad for** Holding yourself back

✦ **Best star partners** Libra

Energy level Gemini: September 2024

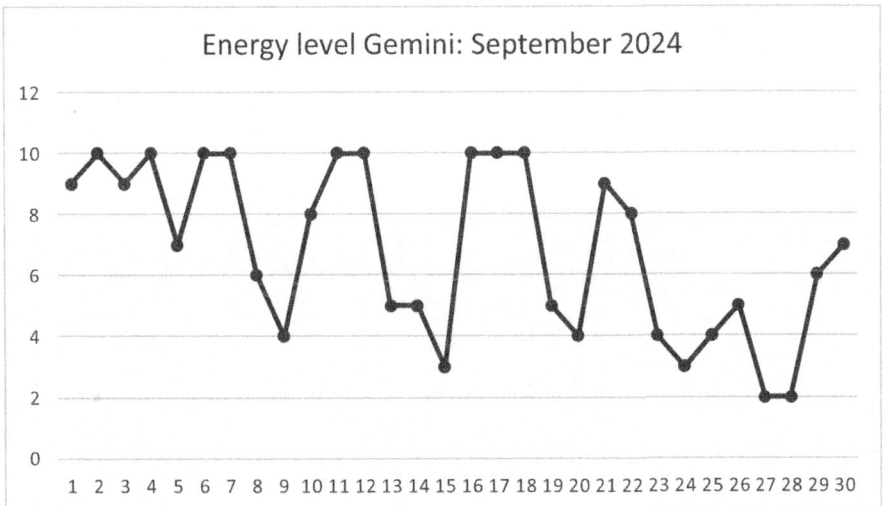

OCTOBER

♥ **Love** As far as love is concerned, you feel a bit like a tiger in a cage, you are restless and nervous, have wanderlust and try to escape this state and somehow satisfy your desire for togetherness. Around the full moon on October 17, there is nothing better than a rendezvous with your old or a new partner, respectively. You will be very happy.

♕ **Success** In October things are going the Gemini way, namely cheerful, fresh, easy, uncomplica-ted - just in your sense. From the 20th on, the cosmic clock points to stress again, but you are fit and even enjoy this chaos.

👍 **Good for** Venus In Scorpio doubles your erotic charisma and Jupiter connects you with the right people.

☹ **Bad for** Always see the downside and not the upside

✦ **Best star partners** Aries, Libra, Sagittarius

Energy level Gemini: October 2024

NOVEMBER

♥ **Love** The full moon on November 15 heralds an interesting time for solo singers: Magical encounters take place, you think you've known each other forever, hot and passionate feelings blaze.

♉ **Success** On the 10th of the month, begins a darn time when hardly anything goes over without stress. It's thanks to your great emotional line that you're still smiling. The last week of November offers a high. Mars and Jupiter are responsible for this, and they really make your hormone levels skyrocket.

👍 **Good for** love, lust and passion

☹ **Bad for** holding oneself back and slowing down

✦ **Best star partners** Libra, Gemini, Aquarius

Energy level Gemini: November 2024

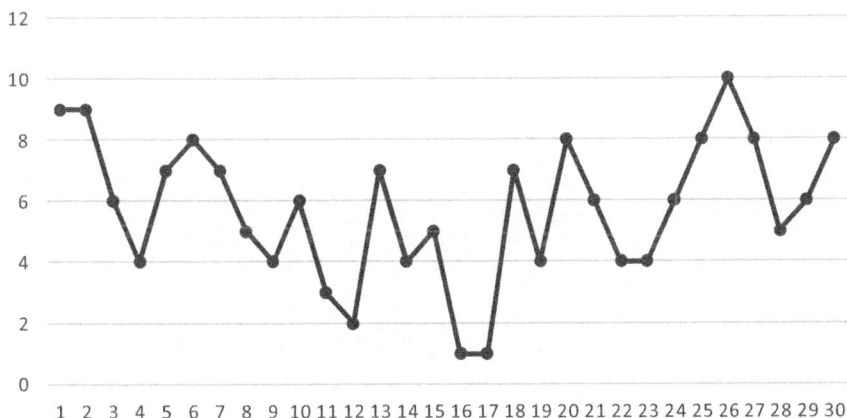

65

DECEMBER

♥ **Love** The stars decide that you are the most beautiful and the best and declare you the erotic star. The more you proclaim this to yourself, the more awesome the time will be. No wish is impossible. You don't have to wait until Christmas Eve to make your wishes either. In December, love is hot and promising all month long.

🏆 **Success** You have too much temper, snap out of it quickly and immediately take everything on the horns that stands in your way. Couldn't you be a little more merciful? The week before Christmas will be a real hammer: Drive carefully, don't talk too much and relax as much as you can!

👍 **Good for** Taking big steps forward and upward

☹ **Bad for** Getting caught up in bad feelings

✦ **Best star partners** Cancer, Leo, Libra

Energy level Gemini: December 2024

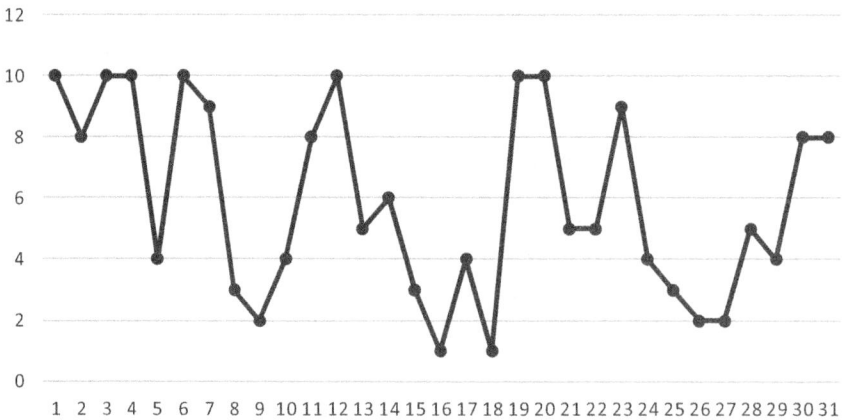

CANCER
(June 22-July 22)

Each sign of the zodiac has a star that guides and directs it. With you it is the moon. It gives you your deep feeling and your great intuition. In 2024 the sun rules, but just as the moon receives its light from the sun in the sky, you will also receive generous gifts from the sun in the coming year. Assuming you have a secure job, for example, you are a civil servant, then you must expect one or the other adversity in the coming year. Why? Because planet Pluto has a strong influence on your zodiac sign. He doesn't want everything to go on as before. On the other hand, you have a great year ahead of you if you are a freelancer, for example, and you have to expect something different to happen every day. Pluto and the Sun make you strong.

In the first half of the year, Jupiter is in a great position. It will guide and accompany you and tell you where there is something to get: More money, more responsibility, more joy of life, Jupiter will take care of them. Saturn is also an important planet for you. It is in a friendly trine to your zodiac sign in 2024.

However, he is in the Pisces section, a water sign. There his guidelines are not as precise as usual. This may sometimes scare you a bit when things go haywire. But in the end, Saturn guarantees a happy ending. In 2024, your stars will mainly benefit those of you who have already retired or are no longer working for some other reason. You are to throw yourself into something new. This can be anything but what you have been doing all your life. Maybe you learn astrology or start another, mediumistic study. Perhaps you press again the school bench in an advanced training course of the adult education center or become a volunteer helper in a social area.

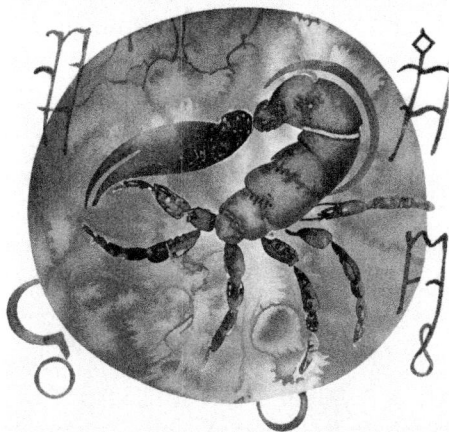

LOVE

The regent of the year, the sun, will conjure you a brilliant year of love with absolute highlights around the full moon. However, this presupposes a harmonious partnership: you love and understand each other, respect each other and don't try to squeeze yourself into some wishful image. Then everything will be even more beautiful. You will feel disagreements more painfully than usual in 2024. Then action must be taken and with the help of Saturn, a professional for such problems, you will succeed in the vast majority of cases. You are single and this possibly already for a long time? Then get in the mood at the beginning of the year that you will find the person who suits you in 2024. Connect with the moon. Whenever it increases, your charisma becomes stronger. Maybe you don't even notice it yourself, but your fellow men certainly do. A magic magnetism goes out from you and draws people in the spell. Automatically, these are those who also suit you. You can therefore calmly get involved when someone addresses you. Around the full moon you should be ready for a meeting. After that you will also know if you fit together or not. Sun

Stars lead, success is felt:
Discover mystical paths!

CAREER

With your great stars you will automatically secure and expand your professional situation. In addition to the Sun's brilliance, you will also be connected to Saturn throughout the year. This star will always come to your aid when things get difficult, problems arise, you get stuck. Saturn awakens a sense of power and reveals ways to attain it. Then, too, there is Jupiter. He embraces your zodiac sign in a friendly sextile. By May 25, you're basically at an advantage, with a good chance of success and more money. That Pluto exerts His influence and under certain circumstances urges you to make a push in a new direction professionally has already been said. The better times are in the first half of the year.

CHARACTER:	Receptive, quiet, friendly
PERSONAL APPEARANCE:	Reserved, caring
FEELING:	Compassionate, intimate
STONE:	Pearl
ANIMAL:	Rabbit
FLOWER:	Water Lily
BEST DAY:	Monday

JANUARY

💜 **Love** In January you receive rather cool waves from Venus, the love planet: there you are already happy if someone lies next to you in bed at night and cuddles with you.

🏆 **Success** January doubles your ambitions. You are not necessarily looking for a title or a promotion. You want to make a difference professionally, to do something that is sustainable and meaningful. If you have been looking for a job for a long time, you can count on planetary support now. You have the bright idea that a company needs.

👍 **Good for** Good for trying

☹ **Bad for** Always doing the same thing

✦ **Best star partners** Pisces, Virgo, Capricorn

Full Moon: 25. 1.

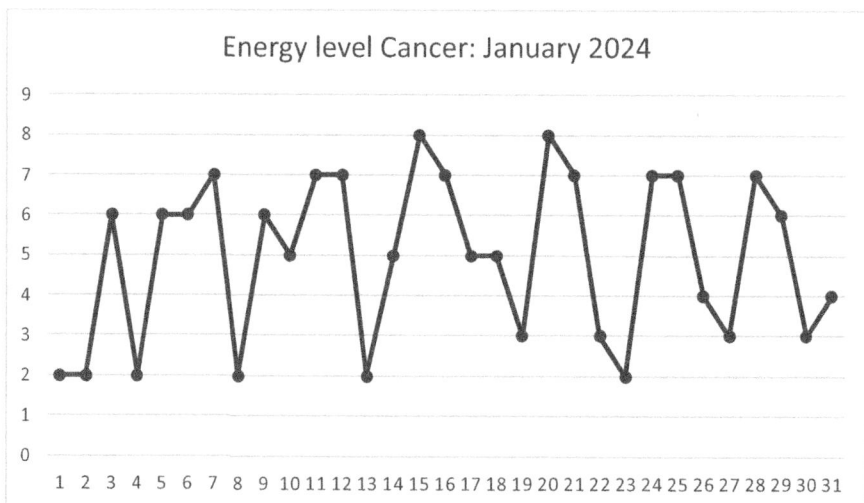

FEBRUARY

♥ **Love** Mars and Venus, who are responsible for love in astrology, stay opposite your zodiac sign in Capricorn until the middle of the month. Feel free to take this as an invitation to devote more time to love. This is true for those of you who are in a partnership, and also if you are currently solo. The second half of the month offers then less amusement.

♕ **Success** Until the 20th the sun stands unfavorably, also other planets do not really support you. Then, from the last ten days, things get better. Now you can even take a professional run at getting ahead. Jupiter helps.

👍 **Good for** More closeness in love life

☹ **Bad for** Letting yourself go

✦ **Best star partners** Pisces, Cancer, Scorpio

Full Moon: 24.2.

Energy level Cancer: February 2024

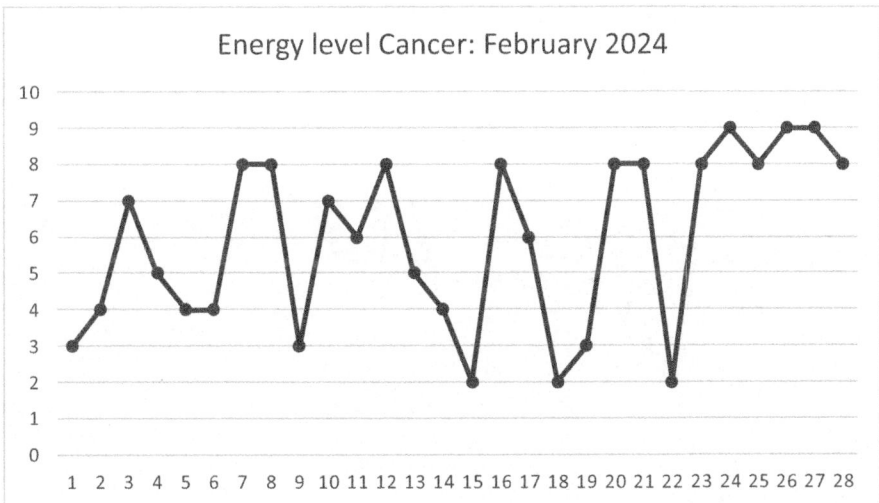

MARCH

💜 **Love** Very pleasant energies come from the Sun. Your heart feels addressed, is happy. However, you will have to wait for love. Only on March 10 Venus moves into a favorable position and invites you to tender hours. On the 23rd you get new love power from Mars. Since it is already spring, you will certainly have one or the other beautiful experience.

🏆 **Success** Maybe you have to work a lot. But otherwise there is little to complain about. In particular, Jupiter and Uranus help you to a favorable account balance. In this respect you are also allowed to risk one or the other in March: You are lucky. If you want to follow the Moon, then you should become active after the New Moon on March 10. The mouth supports you.

👍 **Good for** Business

☹ **Bad for** Gullibility, Childishness

✦ **Best star partners** Taurus, Virgo, Scorpio, Pisces, Cancer

Full Moon: 25.3.

Energy level Cancer: March 2024

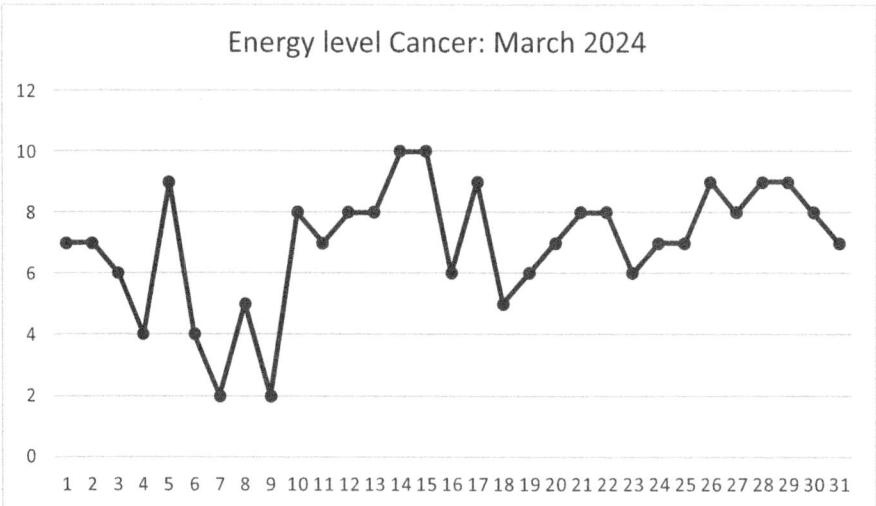

APRIL

💜 **Love** As long as the Sun is in the zodiac sign Aries, that is, until the 20th, you will not find inner peace. But you also know how to deal with it and do something you enjoy. Then, from the 20th, it becomes calmer. The Sun is in Taurus and marches towards Uranus and Jupiter. You can expect surprises there, too

🏆 **Success** Routine is the order of the day, and that you don't let your-self get rattled. Be aware, however, that you have a real package of opportunities at the moment. What that looks like in detail is impossible to say. But assume that something in you wants to be realized.

👍 **Good for** Great interpersonal experiences

☹ **Bad for** Letting yourself go

✦ **Best star partners** Capricorn

Full Moon: 23.4.

Energy level Cancer: April 2024

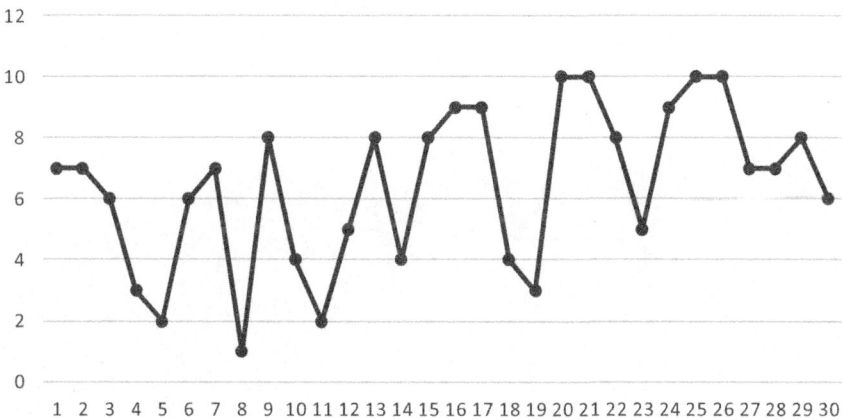

73

MAY

💜 **Love** Venus is at your service until the 20th when it comes to making a good impression. Nevertheless, you will also have to deal with a disappointment or two as Mars moves into an unfavorable position. If you wait until the 20th of the month, the chances for a great love adventure are better.

🏆 **Success** Maybe you are a bit afraid of Uranus. He doesn't fit into your world at all. But if the heavens trust you to handle him, you can be sure it will go well. In May, this Uranus gets support from the Sun, Jupiter, Venus and Mercury. This will definitely lead to new opportunities.

👍 **Good for** Coming up with something that surprises others

☹ **Bad for** Withdrawing when something doesn't work out right away

✨ **Best star partners** Pisces, Cancer, Scorpio, Virgo

Full Moon: 23.5.

Energy level Cancer: May 2024

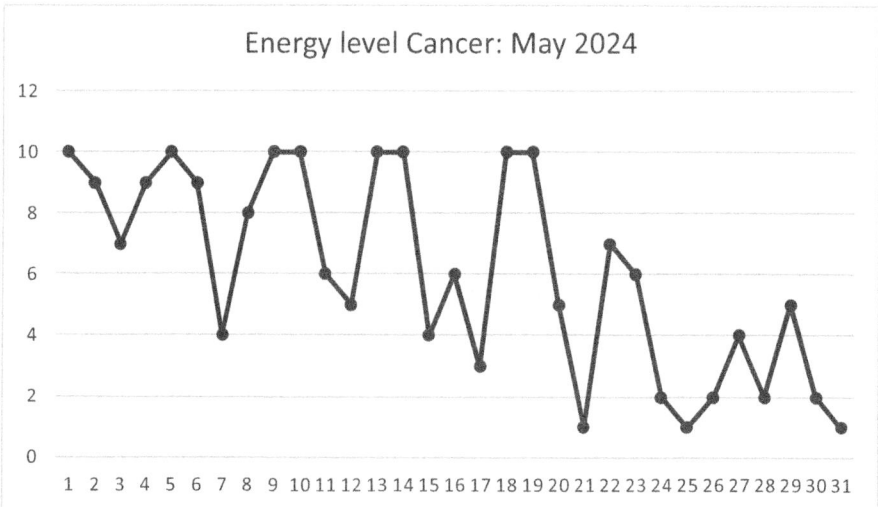

JUNE

💜 **Love** You'll have to wait until the 6th of the month. Then Mars moves into a favorable position to your zodiac sign. Then on the 17th it gets even more awesome, as Venus now makes itself at home in your zodiac sign of Cancer. The combination of Mars and Venus gives you everything you need to be happy in love.

🏆 **Success** Saturn is in the zodiac sign of Pisces all year, and thus in a friendly trine to your zodiac sign. So you have nothing negative to expect from the lord of fate. It will be especially great when Venus, the love planet, marches into your zodiac sign Cancer on June 18.

👍 **Good for** Success

☹ **Bad for** Pretending to be someone else

✦ **Best star partners** Pisces, Cancer, Scorpio

Full Moon: 22.6.

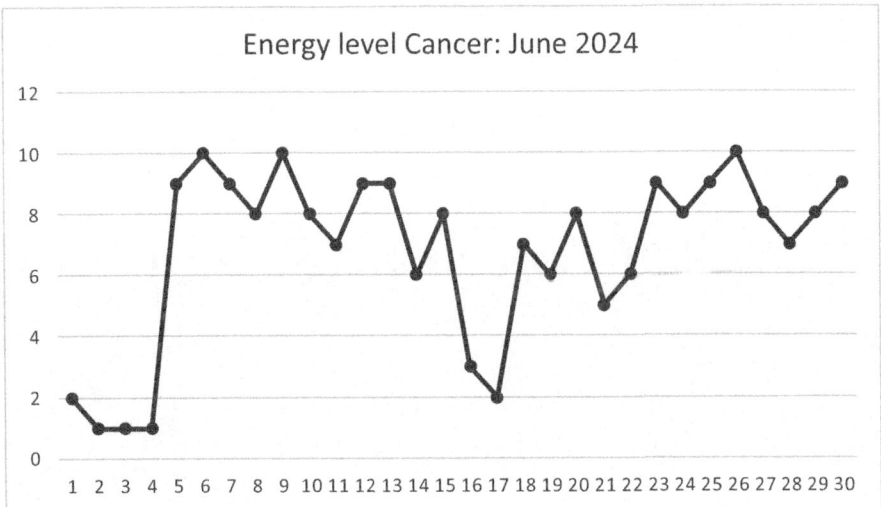

Energy level Cancer: June 2024

JULY

💜 *Love* Until July 12, the Sun and Venus are in your zodiac sign. These stars make it possible for you to not "only" be loved, but also cared for. You will sometimes feel like a baked fish. In the second half of the month you will still get enough strength to get through the rounds well.

🏆 *Success* The Sun moves through your zodiac sign: Your dreams will come true. But don't think only of your personal advantages. The world needs you as a person.

The main thing is that you live your heart. This is especially true for those of you who live alone: Now that the Sun is in your zodiac sign, it is quite certain that you radiate something that is good for the world.

👍 *Good for* Being hesitant, waiting too long, not believing in yourself

☹ *Bad for* Overlooking something important

✦ *Best star partners* Pisces, Taurus, Virgo

Full Moon: 21.7.

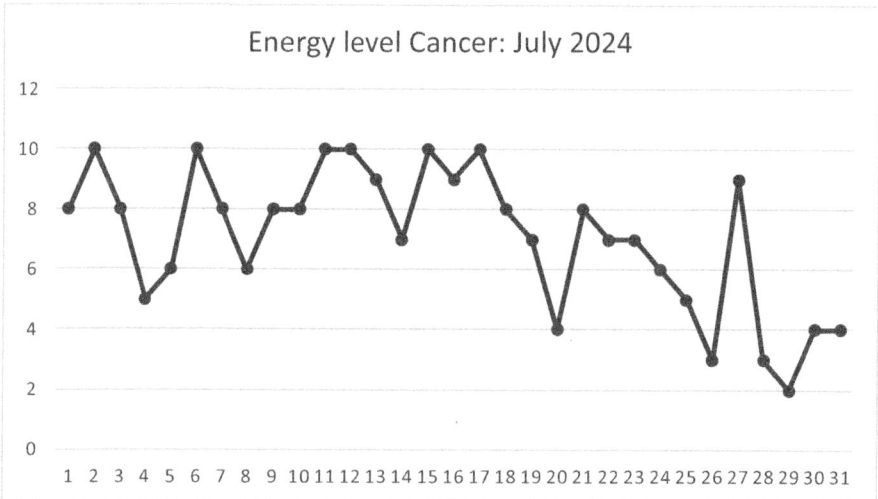

Energy level Cancer: July 2024

AUGUST

♥ **Love** Jupiter and Mars arouse belligerence. So what? Absurdly, your partner ends up glad because he senses that your well-being does not depend on his behavior alone. This relaxation on both sides brings you much closer to love heaven. Singles should be on the lookout in August especially around the full moon. The stars promise that the right one will come into your life.

♕ **Success** The sun rules the new year and thus also the month of August. It gives you a whole new confidence and great trust. Jupiter brings luck, and Pluto awakens passion and love. Of course, the most beautiful would be a journey together around the full moon and in the following week.

👍 **Good for** Success, Money, Love

☹ **Bad for** Doubting Happiness, Doing Nothing

✦ **Best star partners** Virgo, Scorpio, Cancer

Full Moon: 19.8.

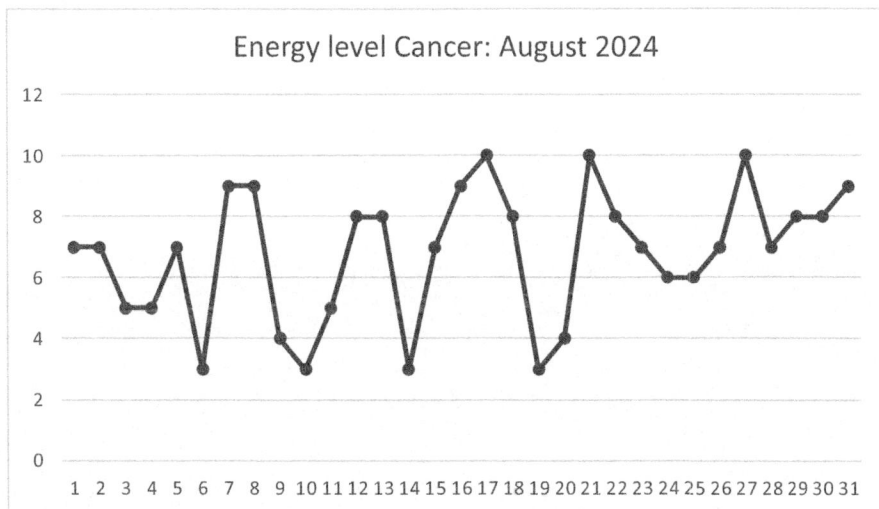

Energy level Cancer: August 2024

SEPTEMBER

💜 **Love** Mars is in your zodiac sign. It is thanks to him and the Sun, the ruler of the year, that you approach the opposite sex unselfconsciously, move confidently and wittily in the social arena, and never miss an opportunity to show yourself. When you become active, great opportunities teem for the singles among you.

🏆 **Success** Mars in your zodiac sign takes you by the hand, doubling your talents and increasing your abilities. It's been a long time since you've had as much fun at work and also in everyday life as you do now. The days after the full moon are most favorable. The waning moon gives you momentum.

👍 **Good for** Accomplishing what is close to your heart

☹ **Bad for** Convenience

✦ **Best star partners** Taurus, Virgo, Capricorn, Scorpio, Cancer

Full Moon: 18.9.

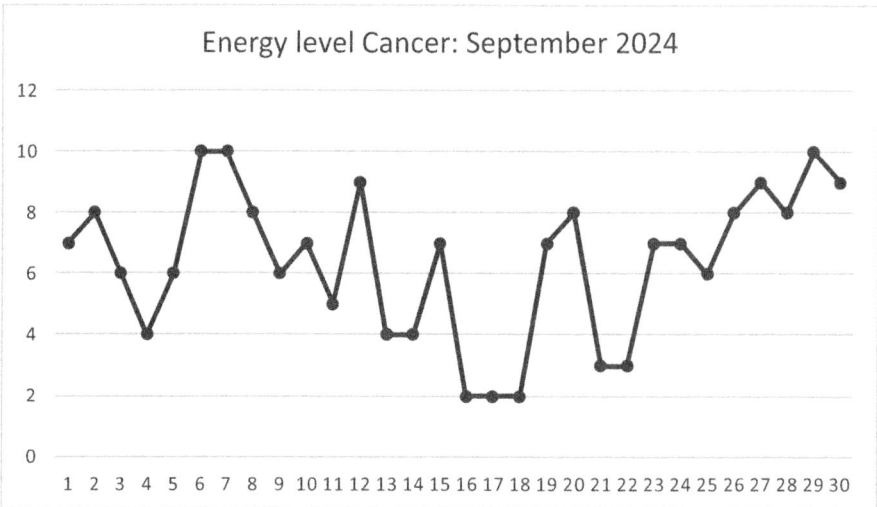

78

OCTOBER

💜 *Love* Autumnal off-season my ass! October brings more eros-wise than spring and summer combined. Only the first week is barren. Starting on the 8th, however, Mars and Venus, two erotic pick-me-ups, awaken deep, delightful, tingling feelings of desire, and you give in to them without any hesitation. Now is also a wonderful time for singles.

🏆 *Success* At work you are provoked, hindered, blocked ...., but you keep your nerve! About October 20, a momentous decision for your future is at hand. It is important that you do not rush anything. Take your time, overcome your impatience, weigh all sides extensively!

👍 *Good for* Believing in yourself

☹ *Bad for* Resigning

✦ *Best star partners* Cancer, Virgo, Scorpio

Full Moon 17.10.

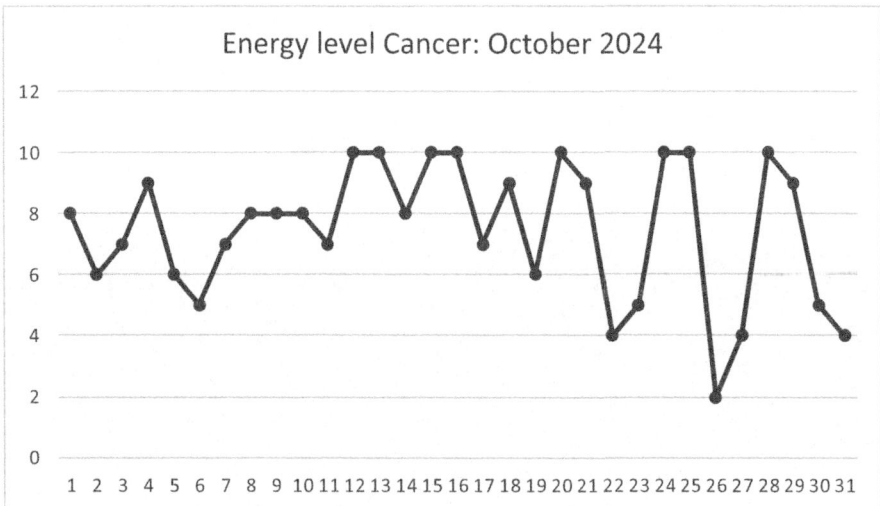

Energy level Cancer: October 2024

79

NOVEMBER

💜 **Love** For the first week of November, the stars promise good news and a friendly face on every day. Even a mad lust experience is in your astro calendar, are you solo, with a stranger, otherwise with your partner. Highlight of this erotic super time runs in the week before the full moon on November 15. You're a star.

🏆 **Success** In November, your genie kitchen works again. You are literally assaulted by flashes of inspiration: How you can become rich and do everything differently. Unfortunately, rose-colored glasses are also involved. Especially be warned against so-called ideas of the century.

👍 **Good for** Success

☹ **Bad for** Being ungrateful and dissatisfied

✦ **Best star partners** Cancer, Virgo, Scorpio

Full Moon 15.11.

Energy level Cancer: November 2024

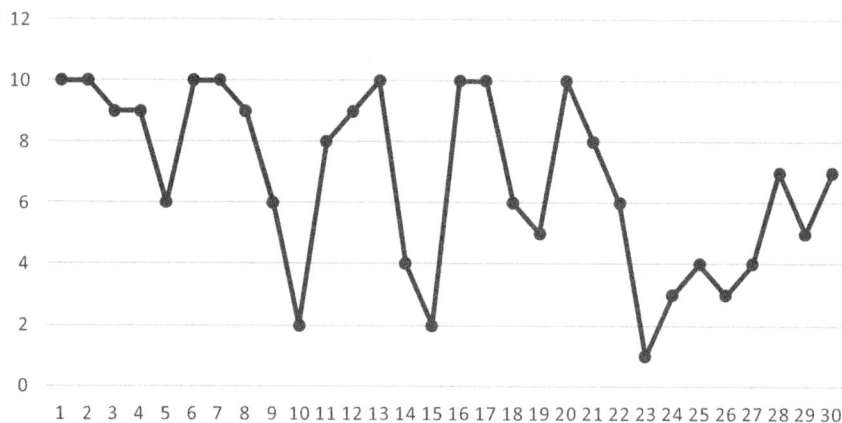

DECEMBER

💜 **Love** Things are looking great for love. The stars even give you a recipe for success: your thoughts have magical power right now. When you focus on someone, you make contact in this way, and they are drawn to you.

🏆 **Success** There is a tendency to frivolity in the week before Christmas. Feel free to be a little picky! You can relax during the last week. Now also runs the best time to prepare for the new year: What are your plans? Maybe you are planning something new. Now you have the best ideas.

👍 **Good for** Embarking on a spiritual path

😞 **Bad for** Living unhealthily

✦ **Best star partners** Pisces, Capricorn, Cancer

Full Moon 15.12.

Energy level Cancer: December 2024

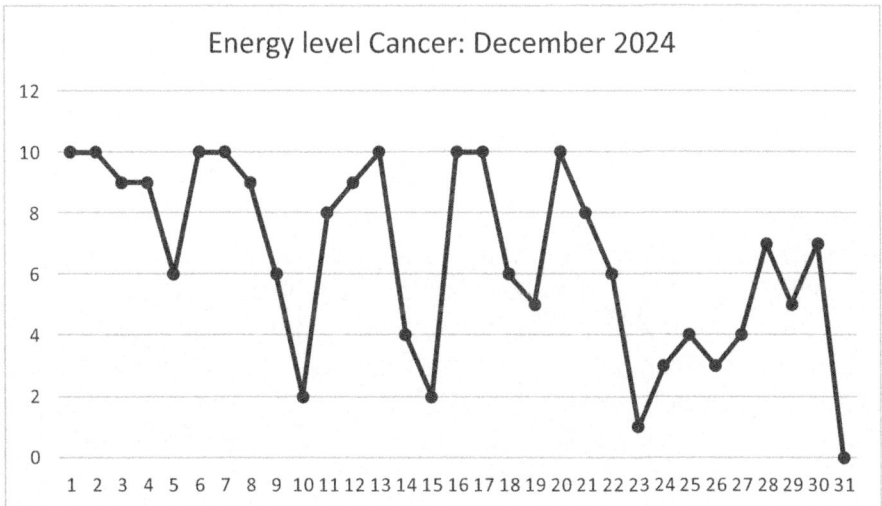

LEO
(July 23-Aug. 23)

In 2024, the Sun is in charge. It is your personal ruler and is therefore particularly fond of you. It's a bit like you're on vacation all year round. You have more fun and more time. Worries and problems, on the other hand, fade into the background. Of course, in 2024 you will also have to go about your various jobs. But even at that, it's nowhere near as stressful as usual.

In addition to benefiting from the Sun as the annual ruler, you'll also benefit from Pluto. This planet has rather hindered you the last 15 years. Probably you haven't even noticed it anymore. At most that you were basically not as happy and satisfied as in the last years. Moreover, from this Pluto also came a susceptibility to health problems. All that is over now. This Pluto is now exactly opposite your zodiac sign. This reawakens your strength. You will be more willing to take risks and sometimes get involved in a story whose outcome is not 100 percent clear. Surely a positive outcome is not always predicted now, but basically you are doing well with this Pluto.

Great support you also get from Jupiter, the lucky planet. He takes a favorable position on May 25 until the end of the year exactly opposite your zodiac sign. As its epithet suggests, this planet promises good opportunities. You can finally be happy more often in 2024. Especially professionally you drive well with this Jupiter. But also, concerning your whole life situation, you can count on its benevolence. This star is especially generous when it comes to love. More on this in the next section. Saturn leaves you alone in 2024. That's pleasant: no downside because you missed something somewhere. But it also means you need to pay better attention to them. Write this down in your daily planner!

LOVE

With the Sun comes fire. More heat arises in your relationships. You lust after each other more and more often. But the effect of the sun is certainly not limited to the bedroom. You also become more enterprising, more imaginative and, most importantly, you are interested in doing more together. This includes talking to each other, exchanging ideas and getting to know each other's hidden sides. What is the reason for this? Because of Pluto. He is now, as already mentioned, opposite your zodiac sign Leo in Aquarius. In the year of the Sun, he can open up spaces that were really walled off in the past: Your longing for intimate togetherness, the joy of exchanging physical feelings, lust and sensuality. What about when you are currently without a partner? There's a surprise in your astrological calendar for the summer. You fall in love with someone very different from you.

What you should also let them know is this: This Pluto doesn't tolerate comfortable compromises. He wants the whole life with all its sides. So if you have become accustomed to a kind of average relationship in the last few years, this Pluto may come knocking on your door and ask if you want it to continue. In individual cases, this Pluto may also cause arguments and, in extreme cases, a breakup.

Sun, Pluto, Jupiter - 2024:
Success, luck, love!

CAREER

Things are also looking good in terms of job and career. Pluto lets you look further than before. This also includes that you get interested in further education. Uranus, on the other hand, makes everything you already know feel a bit boring. In 2024 there is suddenly something in your life that arouses your interest, really electrifies you. This can be an idea, an offer, a vision, a prospect of a new job. Your interest grows stronger and stronger, and in individual cases it comes to a point landing. That is, you start a new professional life. Then, if Jupiter is favorable from June luck, 90 out of 100 Leo-born are in better positions. Even those who have been looking for a job for ages will find it.

CHARACTER:	Generous, demanding
PERSONAL APPEARANCE:	Confident, radiant
FEELING:	Warm, open
STONE:	Heliotrope
TIER:	Peacock
POWER:	Rose
BEST DAY:	Sunday

JANUARY

💜 **Love** Mars is in the zodiac sign Capricorn, Venus in Sagittarius and Jupiter in Taurus. In concrete terms, this means that you feel like togetherness and take much more time for each other, especially if your love is already getting on in years. Singles also want it cuddly, coherent and above all reliable.

🏆 **Success** Saturn manifests in your colleagues and allies especially with your bosses: so you have to expect demands, criticism and warnings. The good thing: If you don't freak out, protest or close down, but do what is asked, suddenly the opposite happens: You are courted, promoted and get more money.

👍 **Good for** New ideas and maybe even steps for your career

😞 **Bad for** Doing too much on your own. Teamwork is the order of the day

✨ **Best star partners** Aquarius

Energy level Leo: January 2024

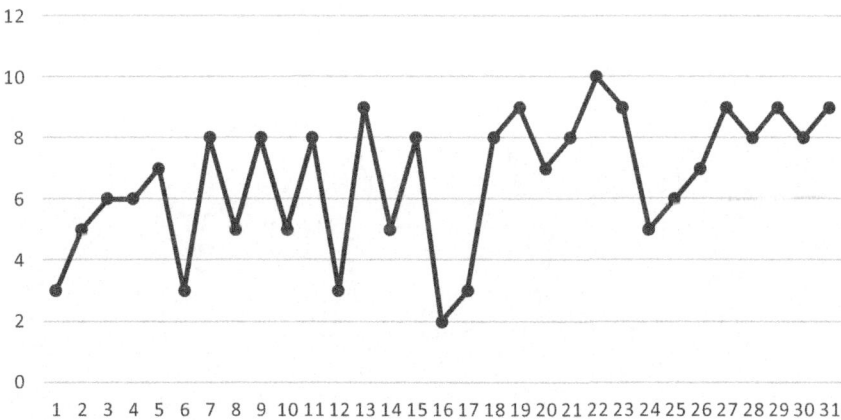

FEBRUARY

💜 **Love** You're bound to have a fun February. But great miracles of love are rather rare. Carnival doesn't have much to offer you either. Mars and Venus, that love duo, stand unfavorably. Only in the second half of the month, they take a better position. Perhaps you catch up now the carnival in quite personal way.

🏆 **Success** The sun and Mercury take position opposite your star sign. There you can already assume a friendly day's events. Major gifts are rare, however.

👍 **Good for** You can now create something that makes you proud.

☹ **Bad for** Ego-allusions have basically no place, and certainly not now.

✦ **Best star partners** Leo

Energy level Leo: February 2024

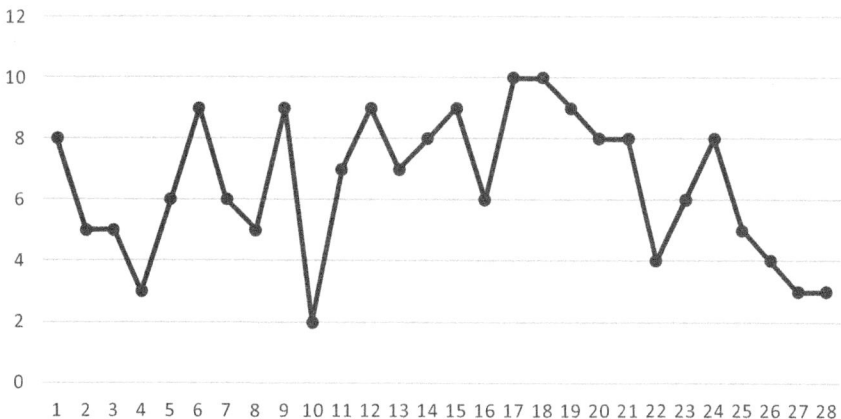

MARCH

💜 *Love* The stars prove bad timing: Until the beginning of spring on the 20th you lack the right desire to indulge in love. After that you would have the right momentum for an adventure, but now you lack the assistance of Mars and Venus.

🏆 *Success* On the one hand you have great stars for an advance, but there is always something missing, so that in the end everything remains the same. What you must not get carried away with is forcing luck. That gives a flop. It is much better to take your time and to feel into yourself. Then you will get hints from the stars. Above all, you will give strength to your soul. This is important because you have many plans for the coming year and need strength.

👍 *Good for* Allowing yourself a treat

☹ *Bad for* Making major purchases

✦ *Best star partners* Leo, Gemini, Aquarius

Energy level Leo: March 2024

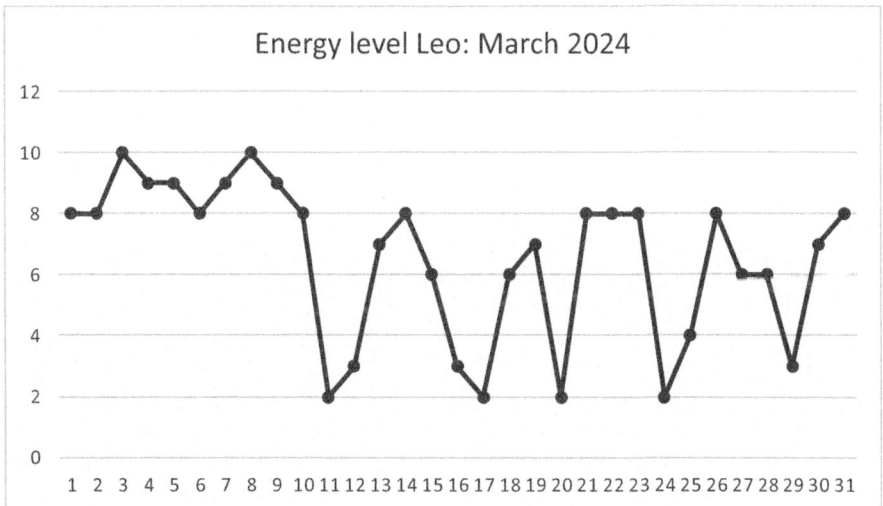

APRIL

♥ *Love* With the Sun and Venus in the zodiac sign of Aries, the first half of the month will certainly not be boring. Some of you may even experience a great love story. Passion will definitely enrich your partner life as well. What you have to take into account is that Mars and Venus, that love duo, do not swing in sync. This means that you have to be considerate of each other.

♕ *Success* Anything that involves work will be experienced oppressively, costing strength and time. Do not let yourself be burdened too much. That would be a shame, because the Sun in Aries also gives you many opportunities. What is important, you should do before the 20th. After that it will be more difficult, cost more time and more strength.

👍 *Good for* Doing something for your health

☹ *Bad for* Sloppiness, also, as far as your body is concerned, are harmful

✦ *Best star partners* Leo, Libra, Aries

Energy level Leo: April 2024

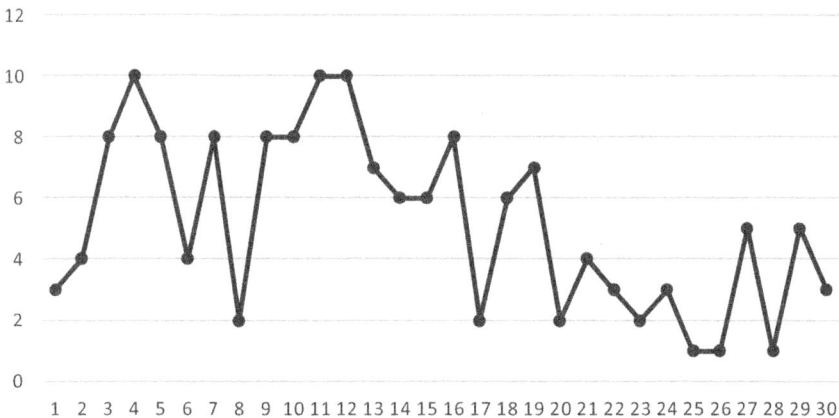

MAY

💜 *Love* Your love life will be very varied in May. Stormy times are as much a part of it as boredom. Good thing is that you can be happy and satisfied even without great star influence. On May 21, the Sun moves into a favorable position. Then, on the 25th, lucky planet Jupiter moves into a position that primarily benefits you: things start looking up from now on.

🏆 *Success* The stars put you under pressure and want you to make more of your life. You cannot ignore this. This only increases the pressure. You have to get over yourself and become active. From further education to retraining, the stars give you the green light. In the last week of the month it gets easier and you get the reward for your efforts.

👍 *Good for* Everything runs better and smoother

☹ *Bad for* Recklessness

✦ *Best star partners* Aquarius, Leo, Libra

Energy level Leo: May 2024

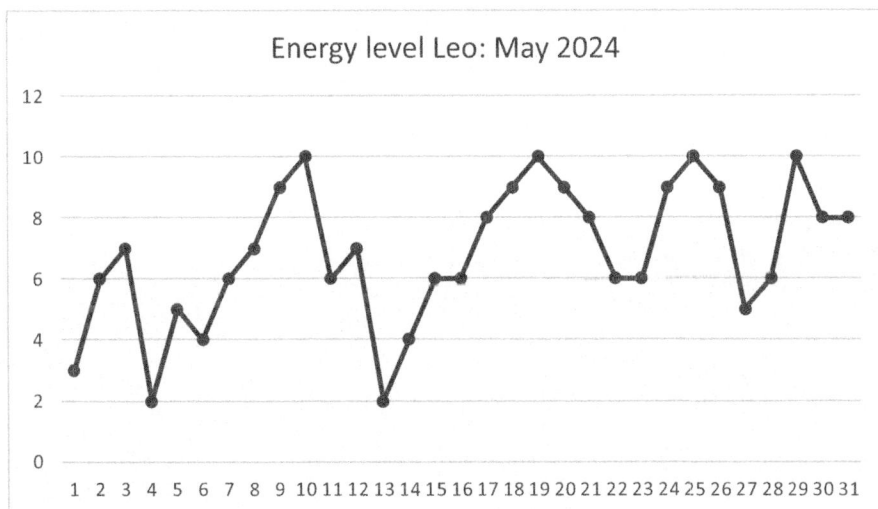

JUNE

💜 *Love* Something wonderful is true for your love life: you will meet a person who is worth getting totally involved with. You will be overcome by the wonderful feeling of having arrived and no longer being alone. In partnerships, it depends on what stage you are in. The most beautiful is when you experience yourself as part of something bigger - a family, a community of souls.

🏆 *Success* Jupiter brings you luck. But, as a Leo, you know this only works if you don't go to work with the ulterior motive that greater commitment is not worth it. The more totally you get involved, the more you want back.

👍 *Good for* Getting ahead professionally

☹ *Bad for* Being dissatisfied

✨ *Best star partners* Leo, Sagittarius, Libra

Energy level Leo: June 2024

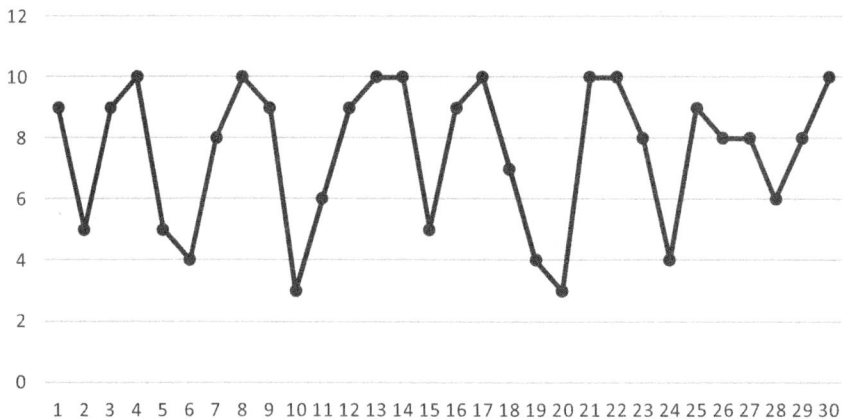

JULY

❤️ **Love** On the 12th of the month Venus enters your star sign. There awaken in you desires like those of a young girl, or young man. You want to taste love - hot, naughty, free and without limits. You will not get enough, neither with flirting, nor with sex. Venus' slogan is as simple as it is stunning: pleasure in abundance! So don't hesitate to always be present where the nicest people are.

🏆 **Success** With Venus in your zodiac sign Leo, your time begins. You are finally coming into your own with your ideas. The world is open to you. Also remember that Pluto is opposite your zodiac sign in Aquarius. He embodies the heritage of your ancestors. Everything that was acquired in the past can now spring up in you like a seed.

👍 **Good for** Happiness and contentment

☹ **Bad for** not being satisfied with what you have

✦ **Best star partners** Libra, Leo, Sagittarius

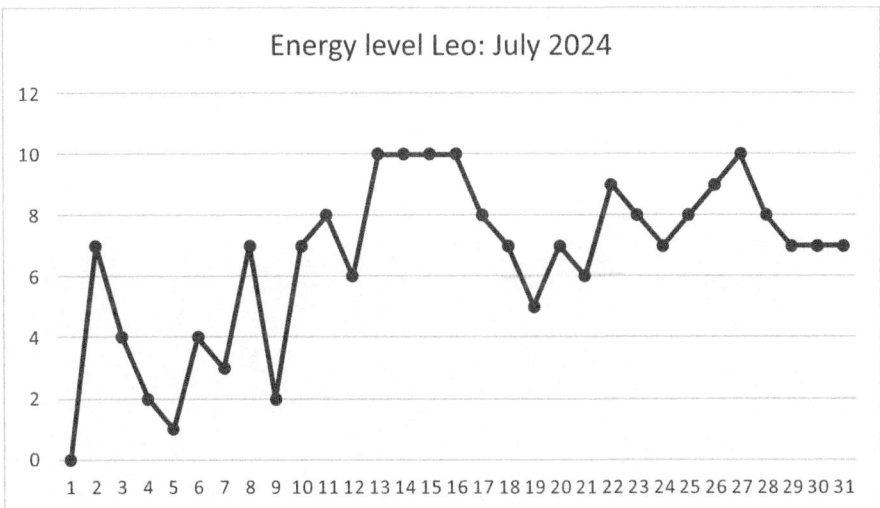

Energy level Leo: July 2024

AUGUST

♥ *Love* Enough talking, now it's time to travel! On vacation, you can surprise each other. Even at home, you can experience your partner anew via joint activities. Take more time for love and therefore for your sweetheart! Common experiences connect lastingly.

♉ *Success* 2024 is ruled by the sun. It is also your personal ruling planet. This not only increases vitality and lust for life, it also brings a new lightness into your life. Bad luck? Crises? Handicaps? All that was yesterday. Now and today comes happiness. In August, the sun moves through your zodiac sign Leo. This will be great.

👍 *Good for* Luck, gain, advantage

☹ *Bad for* Being unhappy

✦ *Best star partners* Leo, Libra, Aries, Aquarius

Energy level Leo: August 2024

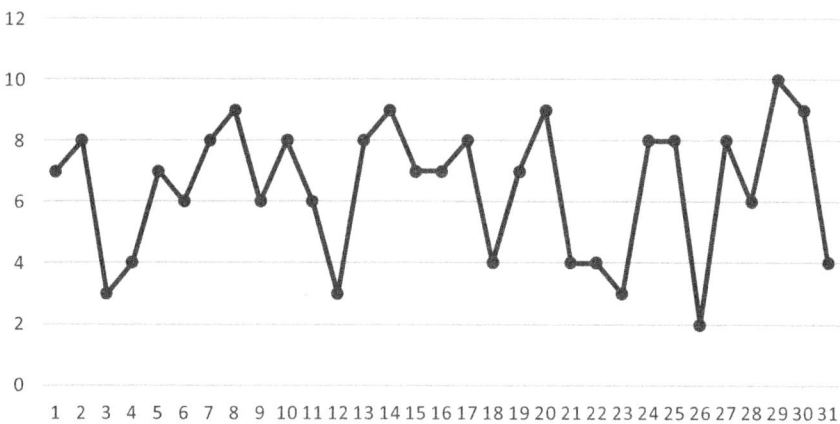

SEPTEMBER

💜 **Love** In September, your love will be tender, romantic and playful. If you take more time for your sweetheart, you will rediscover the fun of togetherness. The fact that you also have sex significantly more often is another consequence of the great stars. Singles also experience a real love high, if you approach potential candidates with an open mind and let yourself be surprised.

🏆 **Success** You have the Sun to thank for a casual equanimity in September. If something doesn't work out right away, try again or change direction in the second step. On top of that, you are more patient, more forgiving with colleagues and bring a lot of wit to the workplace. Where does all this come from? Pluto in your opposite sign Aquarius has his hands in this, too. He virtually shakes you once and brings to light what was hidden and previously unnoticed by you.

👍 **Good for** A pleasant month, maybe even bringing more money

☹ **Bad for** Asking for too much and spending too much money

✨ **Best star partners** Libra, Aquarius, Aries

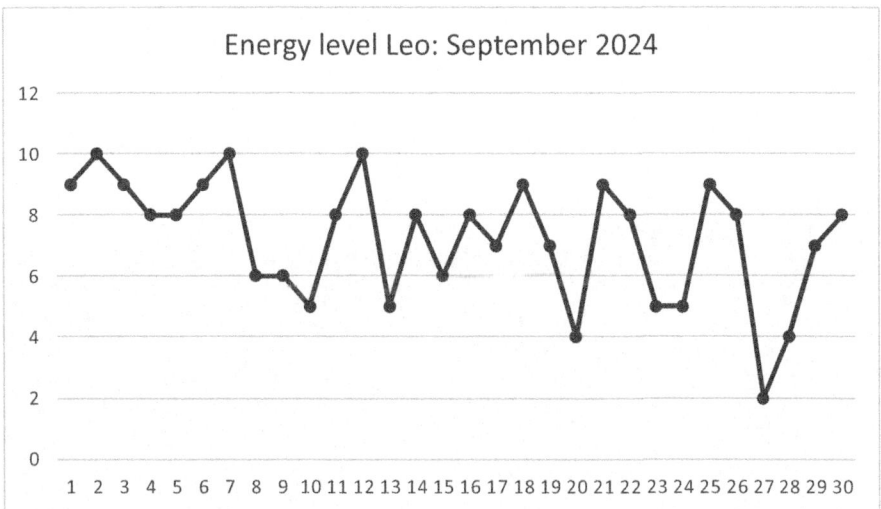

Energy level Leo: September 2024

93

OCTOBER

💜 **Love** You should not expect a "high-fidelity" month. Especially during the first three weeks of October you will hardly get any cosmic assistance. On top of that, your penchant for drama makes an appearance: usually you make the beautiful things even more grandiose, now you build a terrible beast out of every mosquito. On October 19, the love planet Venus moves into a favorable position. This makes you queen or king again.

🏆 **Success** Professionally, your future is at stake. Therefore, you should not let yourself be guided by today, but by tomorrow. You can't avoid a fair amount of work. But your job is fun, and you like earning money because you like spending it even more.

👍 **Good for** Serenity

☹ **Bad for** Pessimism

✦ **Best star partners** Libra, Sagittarius

Energy level Leo: October 2024

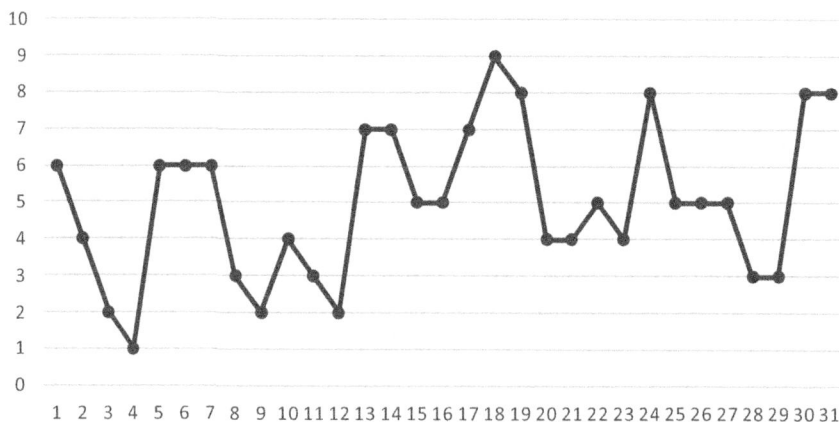

NOVEMBER

♥ **Love** Love is great in the first week of November. It is even possible that, without looking right or left, you will embark on an adventure. That's right! You'll already know when to put the brakes on, and things will settle down from the 10th anyway.

♡ **Success** At the beginning of the month you demand more from your body than it can cope with. The result: You are tired and only manage your workload with groans. You will only be happy and carefree if you allow yourself relaxation phases again and again. What you also have to reckon with are problems that are difficult to cope with. You need time and patience. It is also important to remain optimistic, then, from the second week of November, things will get better and better. Now you can even put highlights on your life.

👍 **Good for** friendships that are worth something

☹ **Bad for** fooling yourself and others

✦ **Best star partners** Leo, Sagittarius, Virgo

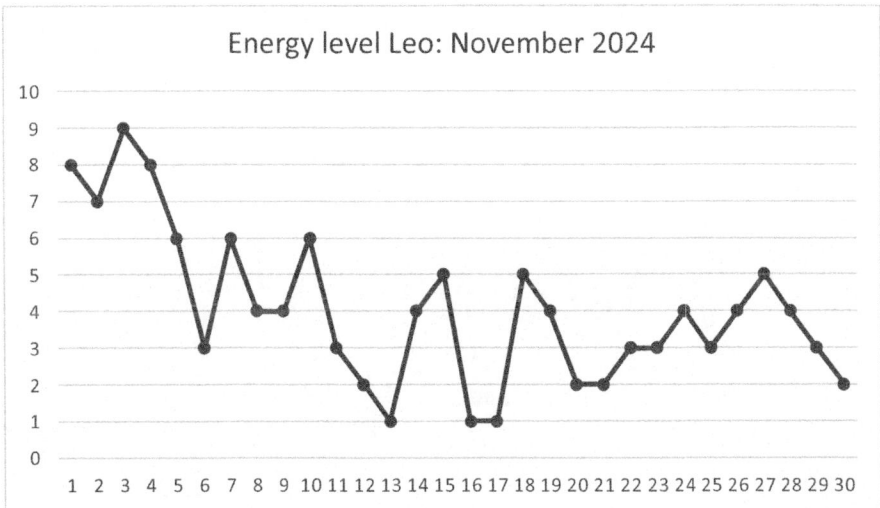

Energy level Leo: November 2024

95

DECEMBER

💜 **Love** Planet Mars moves through your zodiac sign throughout the month, and Venus beams at it from the opposite sign. This gives you a crazy sensuality. Hopefully you won't overshoot the mark with your great power right away, especially don't overtax your partner. That would be a shame and deprive you of a Christmas season you've always dreamed of. The stars signal an intense, passionate time.

🏆 **Success** If you want to get ahead, you need to show you've got it now. The Sun is strong and Mars has settled right into your zodiac sign. No one else has such great stars. Just in time for two days before Christmas, your power stars are aiming further and you can devote yourself fully to love.

👍 **Good for** Getting involved with spiritual things

☹ **Bad for** Forgetting the soul

✦ **Best star partners** Sagittarius, Leo, Libra

Energy level Leo: December 2024

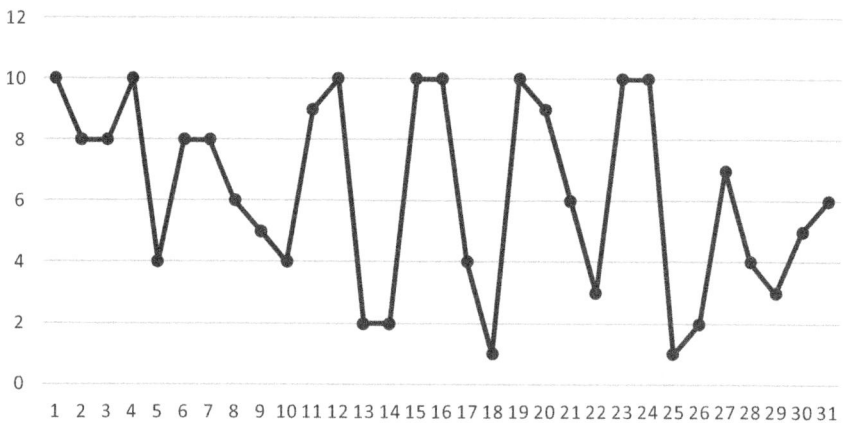

VIRGO
(August 24-September 23)

The coming year is ruled by the sun. Therefore, you can trust life. Your ship of life is gliding along. There is nothing known about storms and other threats. Saturn is opposite your zodiac sign. Basically, you have a good relationship with this planet. Now, when he is opposite your zodiac sign, you can be even more confident. He is watching out that you do not make any mistakes. But unlike otherwise, in 2024 he is downright caring, almost as if you are a child who needs someone by your side. Whenever you lack confidence, when you're not sure, he encourages you. This holds a great opportunity to make more of your life.

Jupiter and Uranus are in your zodiac sign until the end of May. This means that fate will offer you new opportunities. To take up the image of the ship once again, Uranus and Jupiter will take you to whole new lands on your journey during the first five months. In other words, your life will also be exciting and thrilling. Then, starting in June, Jupiter is in the zodiac sign of Gemini. This is tantamount to an invitation. You will now not only get closer to all the people you know, but also make many new friends. You will also get new professional fields in which you will prove yourself.

Neptune also plays an important role. He takes care of a side that you already know. It is hunches, sometimes a very precise knowledge, that the world is not only what you hear and see, but that behind it there is still a medial, mystical world. You will get to know it better and it will open up completely new possibilities for you.

LOVE
You are a down-to-earth and realistic person - but not in love. There you become a dreamer and illusionist. In 2024 Neptune and Saturn are in your partner house. This awakens your desires for a love that touches the sky. In the unfavorable case you experience your current love so little

fulfilling that you separate. In the favorable case you meet the person who makes you happy. Also the possibility exists of course that your present partnership grows, becomes bigger, breaks narrow limits and tastes Se again and again the paradise. You, a Virgo, have a rare chance to have a truly fulfilling love life in 2024. How is it if you have decided to stay single? Wonderful! You will experience everything that makes you happy in your imagination and dreams. Nothing will be missing for you. And how about if you are one of the Virgos thinking of starting a family? Fantastic! In the first half of the year, the stars will help you. If you make the decisive act right away in January, you'll have company in September in the form of another Virgo.

Virgo 2024:
Confidence, success, fulfilled love life

CAREER

Jupiter, the lucky planet, is on your side. It stays in the zodiac sign Taurus until May 25 and will enrich your life. This looks quite like a financial plus. But there's also Uranus hooking up with Jupiter. You'll have to come up with something special. If you want to make it big, you'll have to come up with something new. This could be something practical, like a computer or foreign language course. But you may also find that something completely different is coming up, and you sign up for the alternative practitioner exam or begin training in astrology or body therapy. Whatever you do, in 2024 you have decidedly positive stars for success and more money. There's a but, too. Neptune which, as said, is exactly opposite your star sign, makes not only clear-sighted, but also gullible It is therefore important that you also get out your critical side again and again. Do not let yourself be blinded! Please plan something new for the coming year, a change of career, a new place to live or something appropriate.

CHARACTER	Attentive, conscientious
PERSONAL APPEARANCE:	Modest, prudent, reserved
FEELING:	Caring, easy
STONE:	Agate
ANIMAL:	Persian Cat
PLANT:	Apple Tree
BEST DAY:	Wednesday

JANUARY

💜 *Love* Through Mars in Capricorn you will feel deep happiness when you have mastered a situation together with your partner. Even the singles now instinctively choose those people who are not so easy to crack and act. Why? Because it is exciting to conquer this person.

🏆 *Success* Mars in Capricorn awakens longing for appreciation. Get a lot of that, and money becomes a secondary concern. Dissatisfied Virgos should look for tasks that are sustainable, that end in a result. You need that to measure yourself. Only when you can see what you have achieved, you are satisfied.

👍 *Good for* Accomplishing something

☹ *Bad for* No major undertakings in the first half of the month

✦ *Best star partners* Cancer, Scorpio, Capricorn, Pisces

Energy level Virgo: January 2024

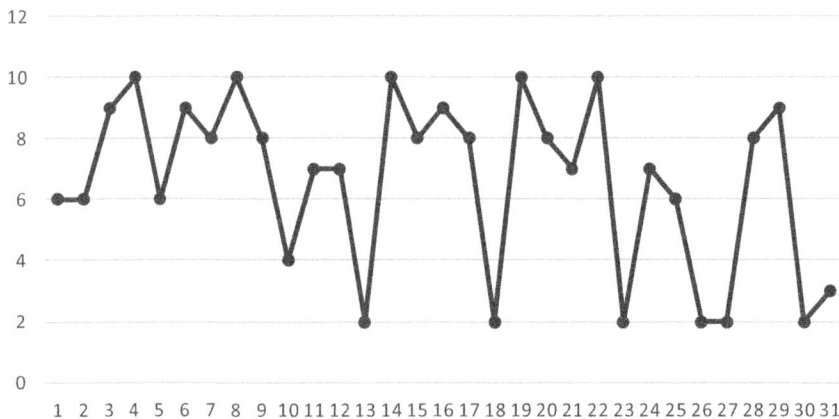

FEBRUARY

Now Pluto is in the zodiac sign Aquarius, where it will stay for 15 years. There is certainly nothing wrong with getting ready for it now: Pluto demands change. It means letting go of habits to make room for something new and better.

💜 *Love* Mars and Venus promise amusement. This doesn't have to be a passionate love story, but be open to merriment and love. In the second half of the month things will be quieter. Now work comes first anyway.

🏆 *Success* Saturn and Neptune oppose your zodiac sign. First of all, routine is required there. This also means that you should not get involved in anything that is not air-tight. On the other hand, the stars could also come up with a surprise.

👍 *Good for* Love

☹ *Bad for* Resisting change

✦ *Best star partners* Pisces, Cancer, Virgo

Energy level Virgo: February 2024

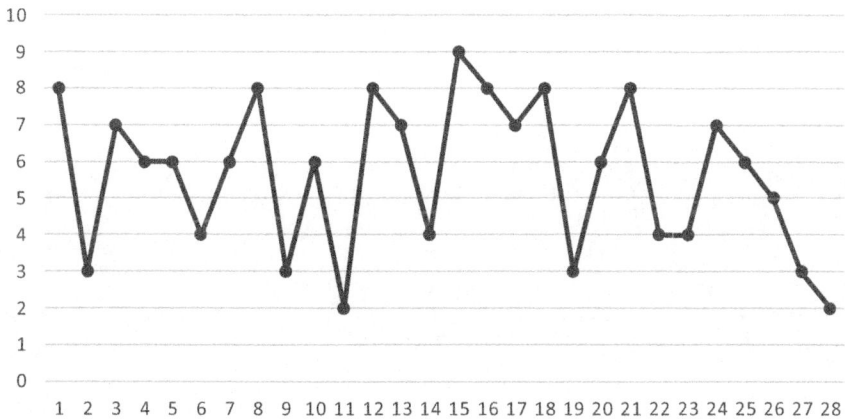

MARCH

❤️ **Love** Love turns you on. You feel like it. But unfortunately the stars are only of limited help to you. Sometimes they do not help you to a suitable partner, then again you have a partner, but no right desire. There you have to wait.

🏆 **Success** Also in your career things don't really work out. Maybe you even have to deal with minor setbacks. Best you don't ask too much, then you can't lose much.

The last ten days of March will be especially difficult. It is best to tell yourself that a time of reflection is called for. This includes not letting problems make you small. Your time is coming.

👍 **Good for** Professional improvements

☹ **Bad for** Legal disputes

✦ **Best star partners** Capricorn, Pisces, Taurus

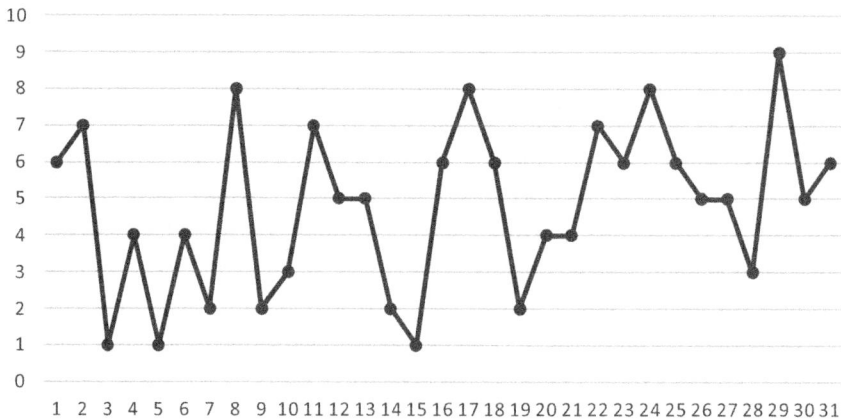

Energy level Virgo: March 2024

APRIL

💜 **Love** Pay attention to who you meet this month: it could be your soul mate. But also take note that relationships too attached to appearances can quickly come to an end, that misunderstandings can easily occur. So: be careful with each other!

🏆 **Success** The way Mars is positioned, you could quickly get the suspicion that you are not being treated fairly. You also find it difficult to stand your ground against competitors. This leaves you with no choice but to be very mindful. From the 20th of the month it gets easier.

👍 **Good for** Standing your ground

☹ **Bad for** Quarrels and arguments

✦ **Best star partners** Pisces, Taurus, Virgo

Energy level Virgo: April 2024

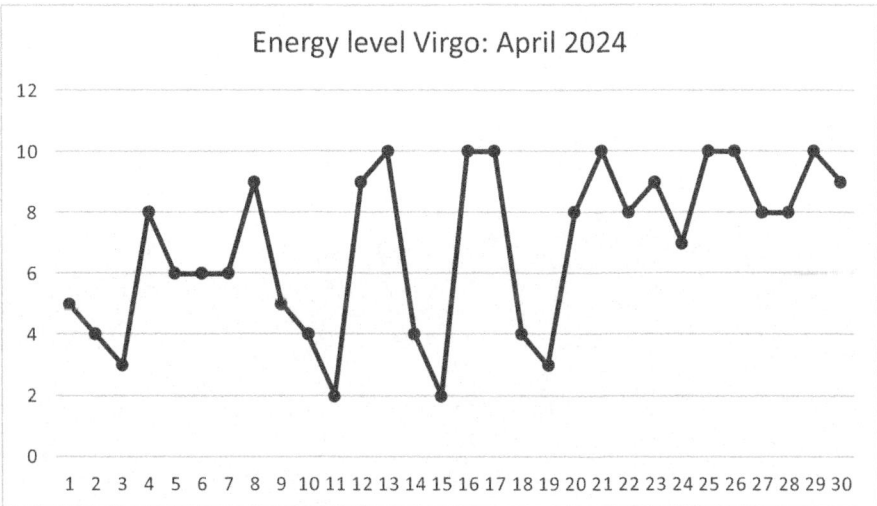

MAY

💜 **Love** Mercury can fully develop and bring you together with the people who are important to you and connects with the Sun, the year's regent. There's a good chance he'll connect the right people. He also helps things get nicer in your partnership.

🏆 **Success** The Sun, Venus, Jupiter, Uranus and Mercury act as a cosmic team to help you get great opportunities. Saturn is opposite your zodiac sign, watching out that you don't overreach yourself with your great opportunities in May. Nice and slow, is his motto, and please, be careful. A surprise awaits you at the end of the month. This will give you a great feeling.

👍 **Good for** Living good for his feelings

☹ **Bad for** Thinking too much

✦ **Best star partners** Pisces, Cancer

Energy level Virgo: May 2024

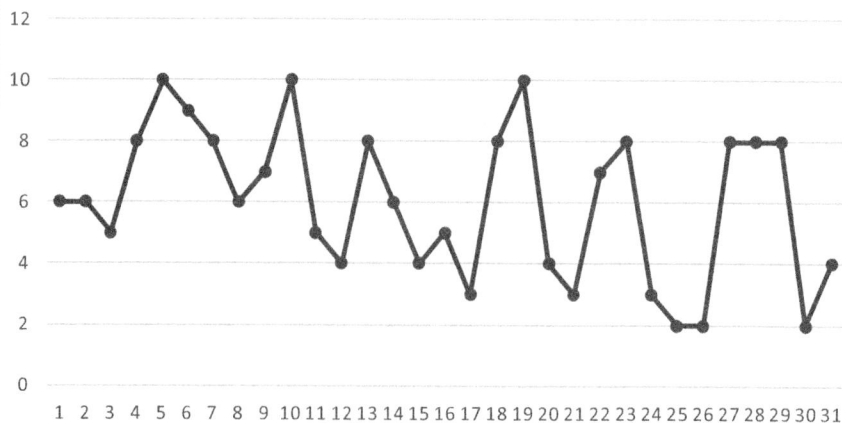

JUNE

❤ **Love** From the second week in June, Mars and later Venus move into friendly relations with your zodiac sign. This leads to more mutual understanding in your relationship. If you are currently single, you can expect interesting encounters. It is quite possible that you may enjoy the summer month of June together as a couple. For some of you June will be the starting month for a lifelong partnership.

♉ **Success** Saturn has the say. It is opposite your zodiac sign. The positive: you grow with the diffi-culties and develop qualities such as tenacity and bite. The first half of the month is especially success-ful. Your strengths are recognized and you are confronted with tailor-made tasks. You come into contact with people who appreciate that you do not give up easily.

👍 **Good for** Self-confidence

☹ **Bad for** Losing yourself in tri-vialities

✦ **Best star partners** Scorpio, Pisces, Taurus

Energy level Virgo: June 2024

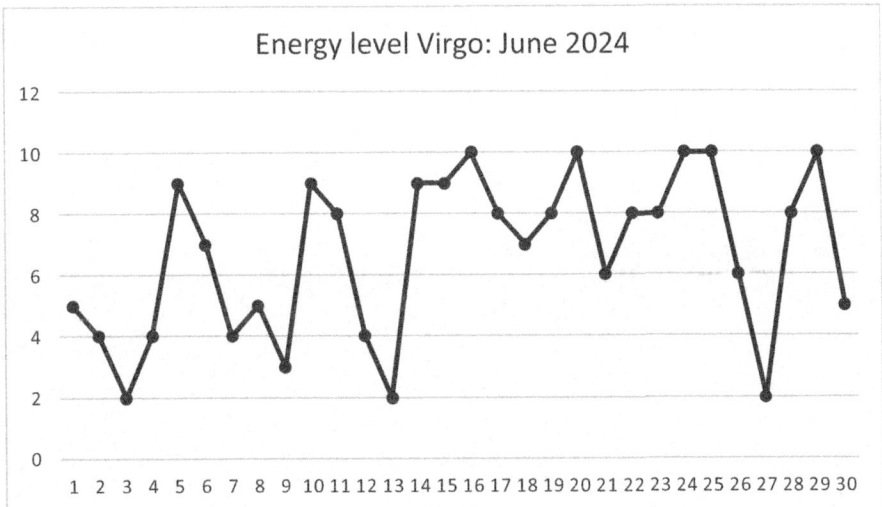

JULY

💜 **Love** There is a warm relationship between your star sign and Venus. Venus gives you inner support, so that you do not lose yourself in life, but always find your way back - like a bird to its nest. It is quite possible that you are dealing with a rival: Don't let yourself be made small, believe in yourself!

🏆 **Success** Your challenge is called Jupiter, which is now in square to your zodiac sign: His message: You don't have to change outwardly, but inwardly. Answer the following questions: What do I want? What can I do? What am I not able to do? They need you to be clear and incorruptible.

👍 **Good for** Friendships

☹ **Bad for** Discouragement

✦ **Best star partners** Cancer, Pisces, Scorpio

Energy level Virgo: July 2024

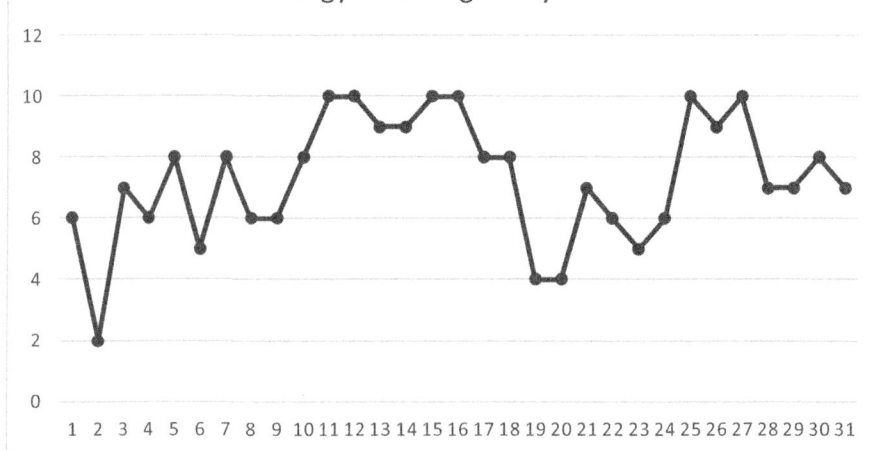

AUGUST

♥ **Love** The love planet Venus is in your zodiac sign and provides you with high spirits. This carries everyone away, even a partner who has become a bit sleepy when it comes to sex. You do a lot together and the experiences weld you together. For the singles among you it is finally announced to be a couple in the future. Should you meet a Capricorn, absolutely hold on!

♈ **Success** Live according to the pleasure principle! Eat what you like and if it is a piece of cream cake. As long as it really tastes good, everything is wonderful. What you enjoy immensely in August: Your garden! You do not have one? Then it's time! Buy pots, plant windows!

👍 **Good for** Satisfaction and happiness

☹ **Bad for** Waiting for better opportunities

✦ **Best star partners** Capricorn, Virgo, Taurus

Energy level Virgo: August 2024

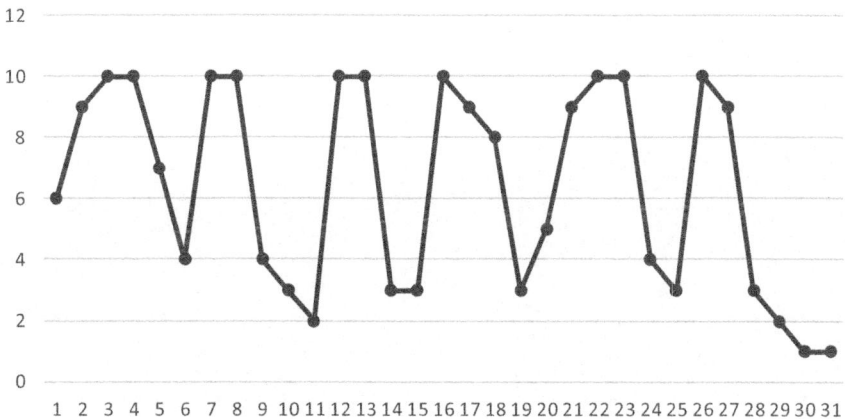

SEPTEMBER

💜 **Love** Mars in Cancer makes you softer, more passive and receptive. You get involved with other people and ARE ready for surprises. Singles therefore have many more chances. Mars also makes it possible for the initiative for a business to come from you.

🏆 **Success** The Sun as the regent of the year is now in your zodiac sign and erases doubts and misgi-vings. You believe in the good and above all in yourself again. This new self-confidence is not only felt by you. When you deal with other people, you feel that you are respected. Especially if you are active in sales, you achieve great success.

👍 **Good for** Taking care of your health

😟 **Bad for** Just letting things go

✦ **Best star partners** Virgo

Energy level Virgo: September 2024

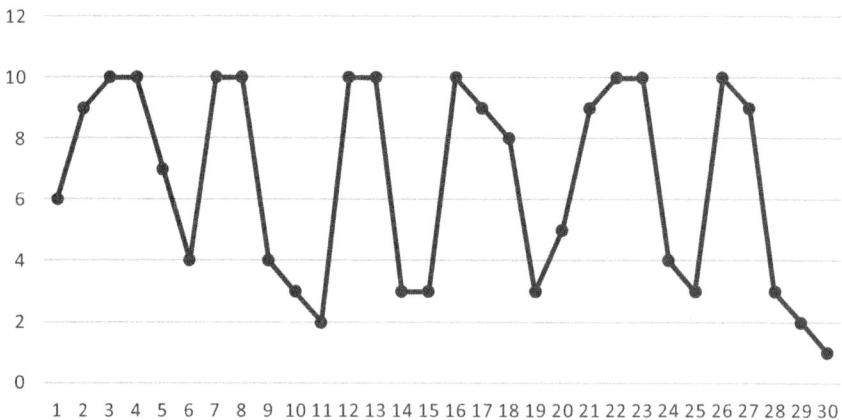

OCTOBER

♥ **Love** A wonderful, sassy, spirited time is going on in October that you can add highlights to if you break out and do something crazy. Also, make sure you surround yourself with the right people! The wrong ones will put the brakes on your fresh momentum. Especially beware of Gemini!

♔ **Success** In October, Mars and Venus are in a sensationally favorable position for you. This will have the same effect as a fresh cell cure: You will be fit, you will feel a zest for action, and you will appear fabulously self-confident. Even the hottest issues will be handled with coolness and ease. However, you should postpone longer lasting agreements until the end of the month; your chances will only get better.

👍 **Good for** love, lust and passion

☹ **Bad for** holding back

✦ **Best star partners** Virgo, Pisces

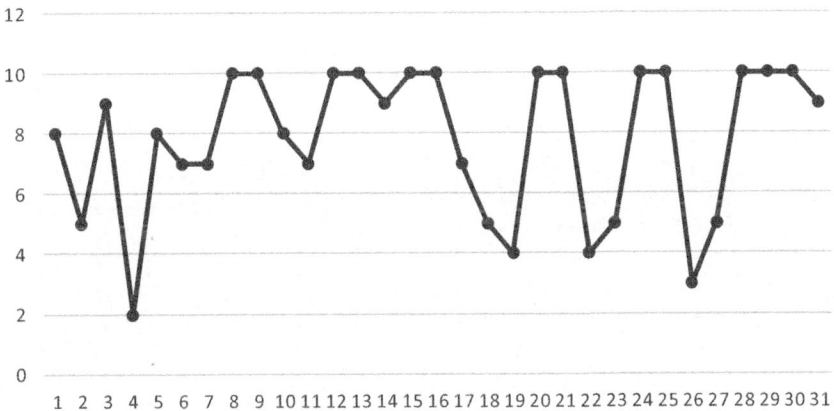

Energy level Virgo: October 2024

NOVEMBER

💜 **Love** Love is glorious, your encounters are light, witty, charming, uplifting. However, this is true only for partnerships that are coherent, which means that each loves the other as they are and makes no demands. Partnerships that are not right at all and have been struggling with each other for a long time may have to come to an end.

🏆 **Success** While others suffer from the dreary November mood, your light-hearted side prevails. Only in the new moon phase around the first of the month a touch of world-weariness grabs you, too. But already from the second week on you are in a good mood again.

👍 **Good for** Erotic charisma

🙁 **Bad for** Always see only the disadvantages and not the advantages

✦ **Best star partners** Taurus, Virgo, Capricorn, Pisces

Energy level Virgo: November 2024

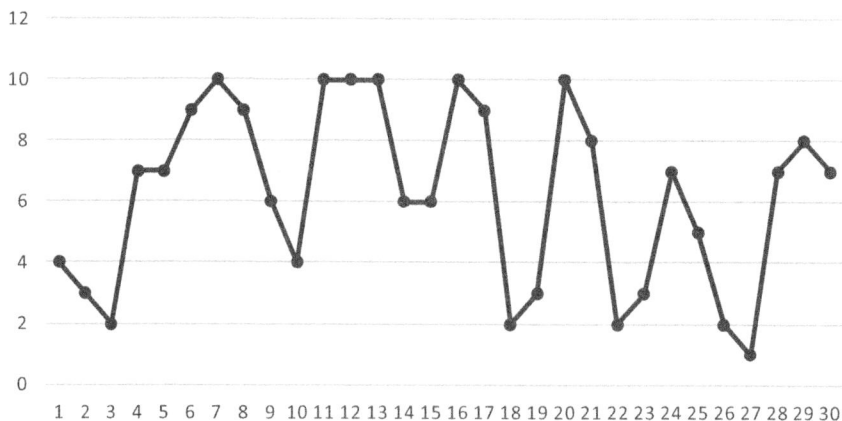

110

DECEMBER

♥ **Love** Just in time for Christmas, your erotic rhythm awakens, and with it a hunger for love, fun, sex and tenderness. Whether you get your money's worth is uncertain. A battle of the sexes is going on between man and woman in the subconscious: there is nagging, nibbling and arguing. Only on the 26th peace returns and you experience an amorous end of the month.

🏆 **Success** You get along with people in general: With your sympathetic nature you even improve your chances in business. After the party it's time to get down to business! A project that you have been carrying around for a long time now has the very best starting conditions.

👍 **Good for** Optimism

☹ **Bad for** Getting caught up in bad feelings

✦ **Best star partners** Cancer, Taurus, Virgo, Scorpio

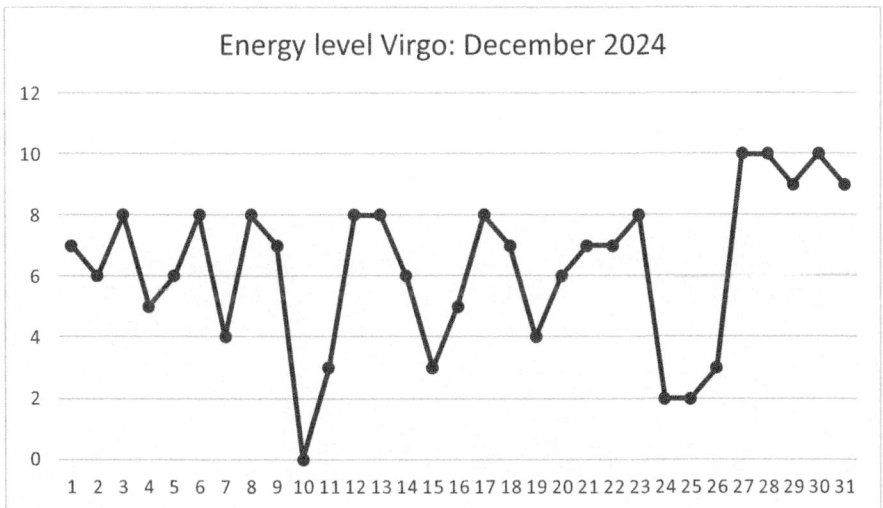

Energy level Virgo: December 2024

111

LIBRA
(September 24-October 23)

The year is ruled by the sun. This means that the beautiful and happy experiences are in the majority. The period from May 26 is especially promising, because Jupiter moves into a position that promises heaps of benefits right away. You will enjoy the positive side of your karma, experience a great love story and professional improvements. The most import-
ant change in the sky concerns Pluto. This planet was in an unfavorable position for fifteen years. In 2024, this is history. Now there is a trine between this planet and your zodiac sign. Thus, all of its positive qualities enter your zodiac sign and thus your life. Pluto is a renewer, in some ways even a revolutionary. Therefore, you can expect that by the end of the coming year you will not be living the same life as you are today. You will be further along, better off, earning more money and working in a better position. But as is always the case with a revolution, before something new comes into being, something old must come to an end. How that will happen in your individual case is difficult to predict. The best case scenario is that change comes easily to you and that you are willing to make it. It becomes problematic when you have to let go of something that is difficult because you have become accustomed to it. However, you can be quite sure that the new one will be better than the old one. It is also not bad if you keep in mind your zodiac sign Libra. It is a beam scale, that is, a tool capable of creating balance. Also terms like balance, middle, harmony are meant. You also try to realize these principles in your life, which leads to the fact that you are basically critical towards changes. This is exactly the point where you are asked: In individual cases, 2024 will also require a greater willingness in this regard at some point.

LOVE
From the end of May the most beautiful time of the whole year begins. A gateway to the land of love opens. Perhaps you do not notice it imme-

diately that a kind of glow emanates from you, a flair of attraction. You certainly notice that the people around you are more interesting and attractive. These are the right conditions to fall in love, to become aware of someone strangely familiar to you. Maybe it happens now that you meet the person who is meant for you. If you are already in a partnership, you will rediscover that you have the right person by your side. However, it is also possible that you are dissatisfied. In that case, changes are called for here as well. You need to talk to each other. In extreme cases it can also go so far that you separate. Of course, this is then connected with problems. But you will certainly be comforted to hear that you will easily find a new partner in the second half of the year. That is also possible that you will feel the desire to consolidate your partnership in 2024, for example by a marriage contract. And also that is announced that you provide for offspring.

"Mystical balance:
Success, love and transformation await"

CAREER

That the sun rules and gives you many advantages, you notice only really at the end of May, and you experience a wonderful, later spring. Professional successes come easily to you. Chance" will bring you together with people who will help you professionally. You may also come across an interesting offer and change jobs. Financial benefits will start coming in the summer. You will definitely end the year better than you started it. However, this assumes that you are ready for Pluto. As mentioned, he is a revolutionary, and change certainly doesn't automatically stop at your current professional situation. But isn't it true that you have been noticing for some time that changes are already taking place or are in the offing? In 2024 this trend continues and concerns in particular you, the Libra. But, and this has also been said, you are somewhat shy in this respect and resist new things. Perhaps you will counter this attitude by a ritual right on New Year's Eve. Light a candle and pledge to the cosmos that you are ready to get involved with Pluto.

CHARACTER:	Graceful, kind
PERSONAL APPEARANCE:	Stylish, courteous
FEELING:	Empathetic, harmonious
STONE:	Sapphire
ANIMAL:	Butterfly
POWER:	Violet
BEST DAY:	Friday

JANUARY

💜 *Love* With Venus in Capricorn, hot adventures tend to take a back seat. You only get involved if there is hope that it could become something solid. Venus in Sagittarius on the other hand makes you want to travel. The most beautiful would be a trip to the south, of course. But also a weekend in the mountains for skiing would be just right.

🏆 *Success* The greatest luck is that you have success. Simply because you define success different-ly. You are looking for new challenges. You want to make a difference, to get something going that is new in your life. This is exactly the recipe you use to amaze the competition and come out the winner at the end.

👍 *Good for* New ideas and maybe even for your career

☹ *Bad for* Doing too much on your own. Teamwork is the order of the day.

✦ *Best star partners* Aquarius

Energy level Libra: January 2024

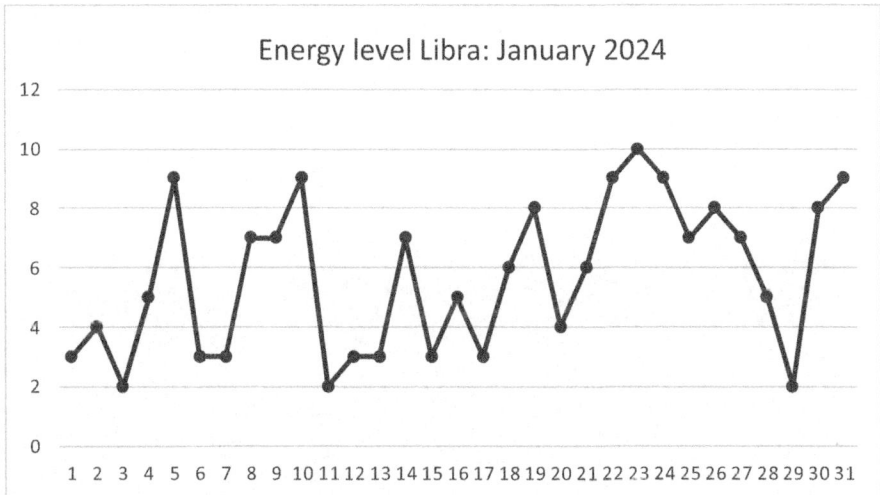

FEBRUARY

Now Pluto is in the zodiac sign Aquarius, where it will stay for almost 20 years. So it's certainly not wrong to get ready for it now: Pluto demands change. It means letting go of habits to make way for something new and better.

💜 *Love* You get the green light for Carnival. Just don't expect a great love story. For that the suitable stars are missing. The second half of the month will be very pleasant in interpersonal matters. Maybe you will fall in love only now.

💜 *Success* The month demanded routine, however, also leaves room for a surprise. So be open and ready to try something new once again. However, there is nothing about financial gains in the stars' timetable.

👍 *Good for* Positive self-esteem

☹ *Bad for* Blue Eyes

✦ *Best star partners* Aquarius, Aries, Libra

Energy level Libra: February 2024

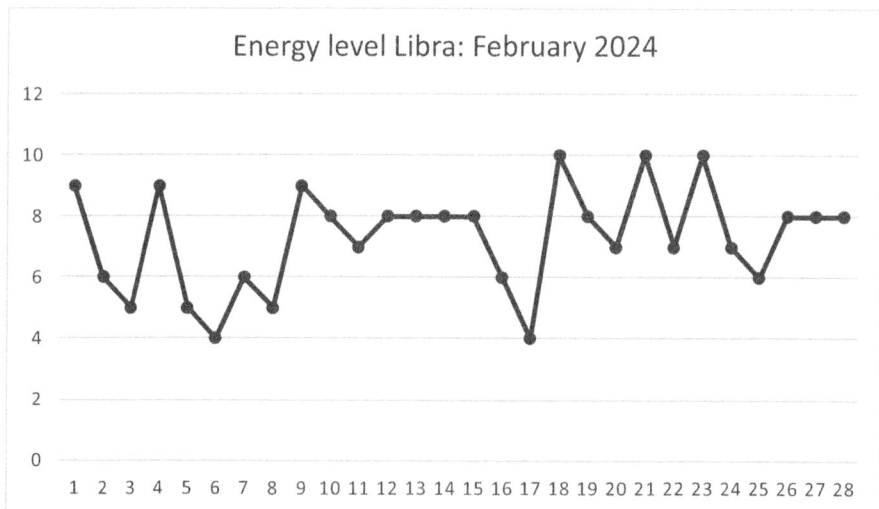

MARCH

💜 **Love** Mars and Venus turn you on. That's when your relationships will be heavenly beautiful in March, with highlights in the first week. Unfortunately, the good mood doesn't last until the beginning of spring on March 20. On the contrary, now the positive influences of the love stars even decrease. But, you put up with that, because you know that it will soon get better again.

🏆 **Success** On March 20, spring officially begins, but your personal spring already starts at the beginning of the month: you get green all along the line for an advance in terms of career. Then, after the actual start of spring on the 20th, the stars even advise you to hold back.

👍 **Good for** You discover completely new sides to your partner

☹ **Bad for** Dispute

✦ **Best star partners** Libra, Aries, Gemini

Energy level Libra: March 2024

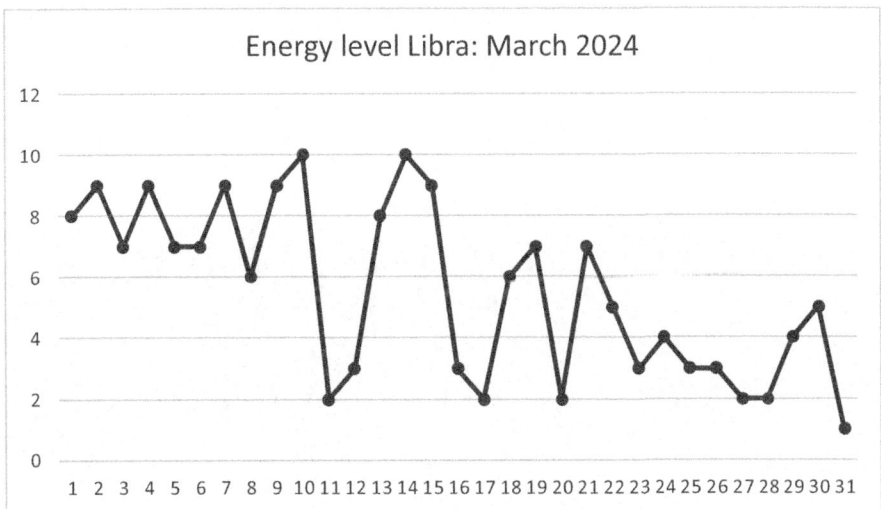

APRIL

❤️ *Love* Love benefits from the fact that Sun and Venus are exactly opposite your star sign in Aries. There life becomes lustful and is full of great surprises. Boredom is a foreign word. Just don't forget that Neptune has entered your life and demands depth and spirituality.

♆ *Success* With your stars, you can accomplish anything you set your mind to. Nothing is impossible because you have many important stars on your side. This smells like more money and a better job. Now you just have to hit the brakes in time: After all, on the 20th of the month the sun leaves its favorable position. Now you have to be careful.

👍 *Good for* All important matters

☹ *Bad for* Self-doubt

✦ *Best star partners* Aquarius, Gemini

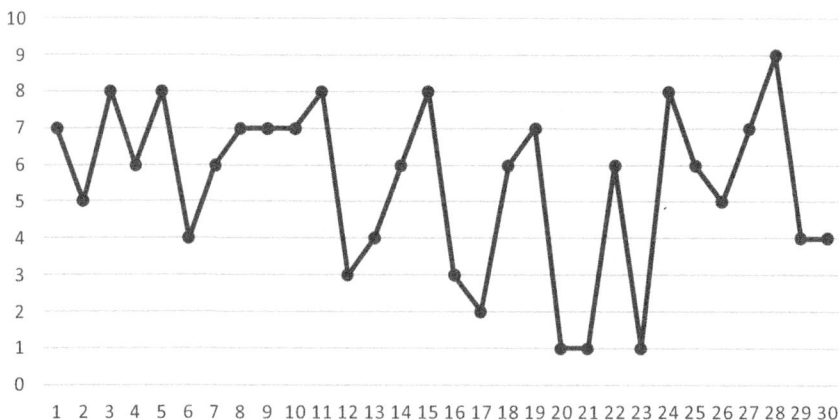

Energy level Libra: April 2024

MAY

💜 **Love** The fire planet Mars gives you a lot of energy. Now, however, you are a Libra, which takes its time. When pushed, you get nervous and end up making decisions that aren't ideal. What can you do? Insist that you need your time to make good decisions. On the other hand, try to dissipate Mars' energy elsewhere, such as by exercising more.

🏆 **Success** In May, the name of the game is to be down to earth. The Sun is in Taurus, a sign of thoroughness, security and love. Let this guide you in everything you do. So you will definitely not undertake anything that is not completely safe.

👍 **Good for** General acceleration

🙁 **Bad for** Letting yourself go

✦ **Best star partners** Aquarius, Gemini

Energy level Libra: May 2024

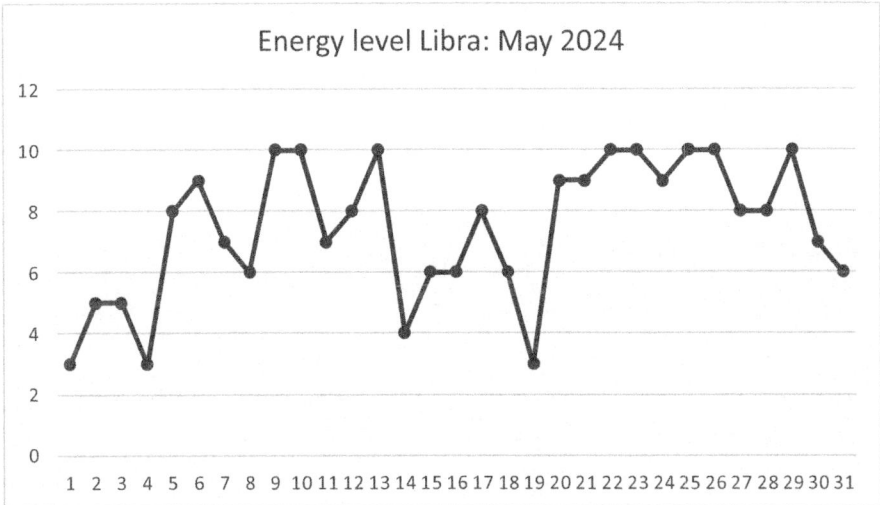

JUNE

💜 **Love** Jupiter, Mercury, the Sun and Venus are opposite your zodiac sign. This means that the month of June has the very best prospects for a grandiose emotional cinema that is as passionate as it is unreasonable. Because not only your heart stops during this mad love, also your head stops thinking. The prognosis: an initially brief and intense amour fou turns into an alliance for life.

🏆 **Success** Your career stars work from the first day of the month. Jupiter inspires you and Mars awakens a desire for power: success becomes almost a matter of course. Even lots of extra work can't take away your desire. And it won't be as hard and joyless as in the past time anyway.

👍 **Good for** Successes down the line

☹ **Bad for** rash starts

✦ **Best star partners** Gemini, Libra, Aries

Energy level Libra: June 2024

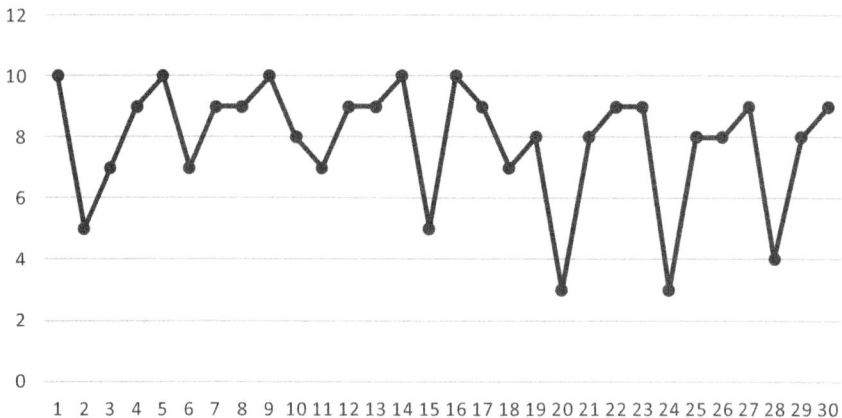

JULY

❤️ **Love** Jupiter in the sign Gemini in your fifth solar house not only ensures that you are beautiful(er) and attractive(er). It also makes for great bargains. Around the full moon, which is the 21st of the month, you also feel more love. The stars even rumor that many a Libra couple is thinking of getting married. The best time would be in the second half of the month.

🏆 **Success** Saturn is unfavorable to your zodiac sign. Something needs to be done about it but then with Jupiter in trine, you can really get things done. Jupiter takes care of good ideas, and Saturn takes care of the realization. The stars are quite sure: Things are looking up.

👍 **Good for** Meeting your soul mate.

☹️ **Bad for** Neptune and thus not heeding spiritual paths

✦ **Best star partners** Aries, Libra, Sagittarius

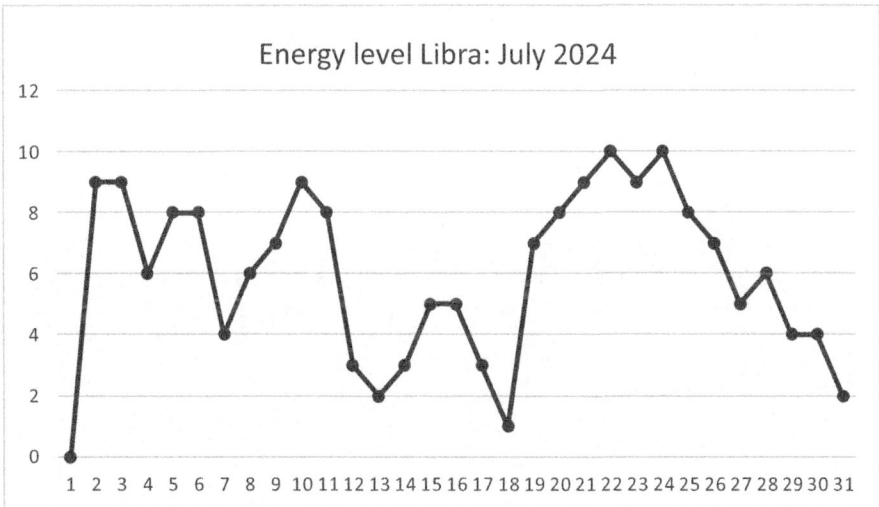

Energy level Libra: July 2024

AUGUST

💜 **Love** The best thing is that you are spared disappointment in August. If you feel love, you can let yourself fall. There will be no more rude awakenings. Sometimes you will also get to feel Pluto. He may interfere with your dream life. However it is, Pluto has the following message: your love is stronger than anything else.

🏆 **Success** Your career prospects are also so rosy that you have nothing to worry about. Jupiter and Mars are both in a friendly trine to your zodiac sign. This gives you a lot of points. There is also more money in store for you at the end of the month. There is even talk of Libra-born among lottery winners.

👍 **Good for** Relaxing, having a good time

☹ **Bad for** Worrying

✦ **Best star partners** Aquarius, Gemini

Energy level Libra: August 2024

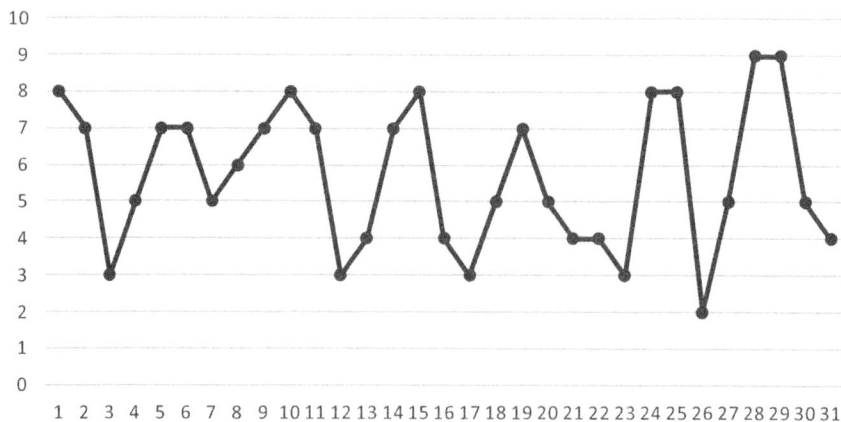

SEPTEMBER

💜 **Love** Venus is in your zodiac sign. If someone is particularly close to you then, it can happen that you seriously think about a common future. Singles really test who fits best and are extremely choosy. Because one thing is also clear: you could also be alone. It's similar with couples. You don't continue to define your happiness in terms of the relationship. You are closest to yourself.

🏆 **Success** Now your dreams will finally come true! Your ideas and talents can grow, develop, will bear fruit. That sounds great. It is. But you also have to believe in yourself. Why not get up in the morning and tell yourself that you will have a successful day today!

👍 **Good for** Venus creates obligations

☹ **Bad for** Hesitant waiting, not being able to decide.

✦ **Best star partners** Libra, Aquarius, Leo

Energy level Libra: September 2024

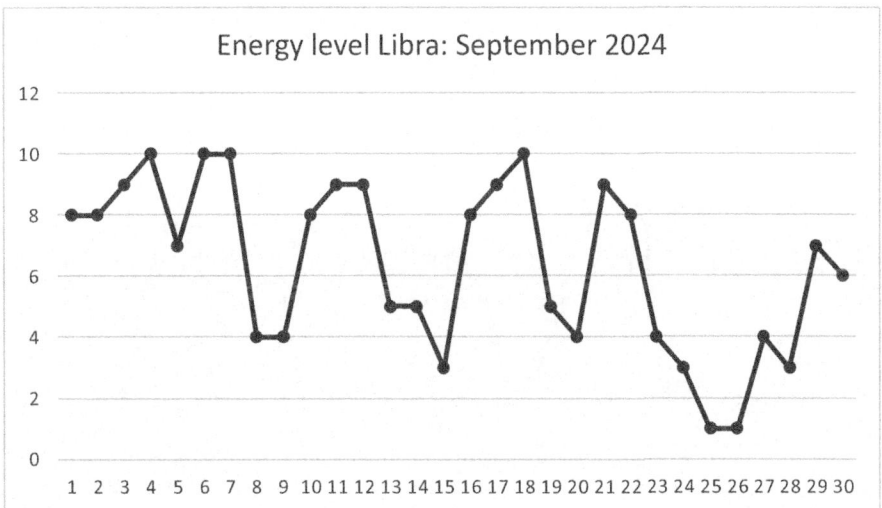

OCTOBER

💜 **Love** Love creates conflicts: freedom or surrender? More towards autonomy? Or is the solution more togetherness? In individual cases, fierce relationship wrangling cannot be avoided. Particularly allergic times are in the third week of November.

🏆 **Success** Everything goes easily and loosely from the hand. You are met with open arms. Luck is on your side. Wonderful, in October stress is a foreign word for you for once! On the last ten days it sometimes becomes burdensome, occasionally even hard; but help always comes at the right time. The end of the month will be bitter - unless you can sweeten it with a trip.

👍 **Good for** Staying positive.

☹ **Bad for** Not letting go of misfortune

✨ **Best star partners** Aquarius, Aries, Libra

Energy level Libra: October 2024

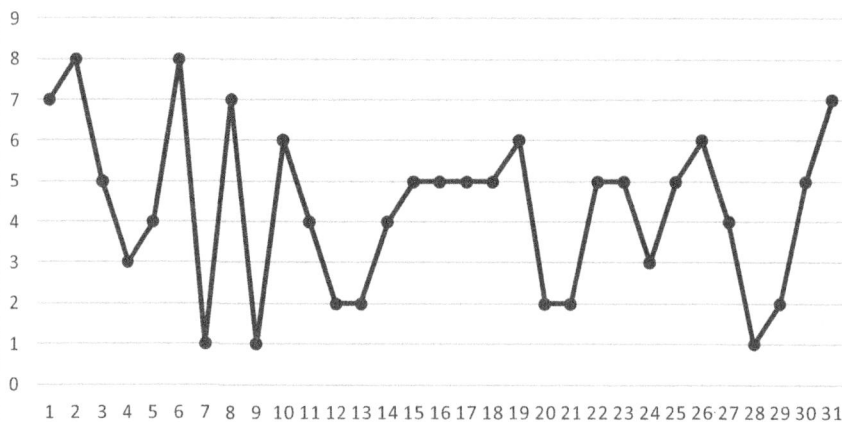

124

NOVEMBER

💜 **Love** At the beginning of the month, love gives you strength. Possibly even a small sensation in the realm of the senses is in the offing. From the 10th of the month it is over with the great prospects in love. But do not let it pull you down. That will change again.

♕ **Success** Until the 20th of the month you have to comb through a thicket of work and handicaps like a bulldozer. But - and this alone is important to you - you are accomplishing what you set out to do. In individual cases, this could also include starting a completely new job that suits you much better.

👍 **Good for** Love

☹ **Bad for** Wanting too much

✦ **Best star partners** Libra, Leo

Energy level Libra: November 2024

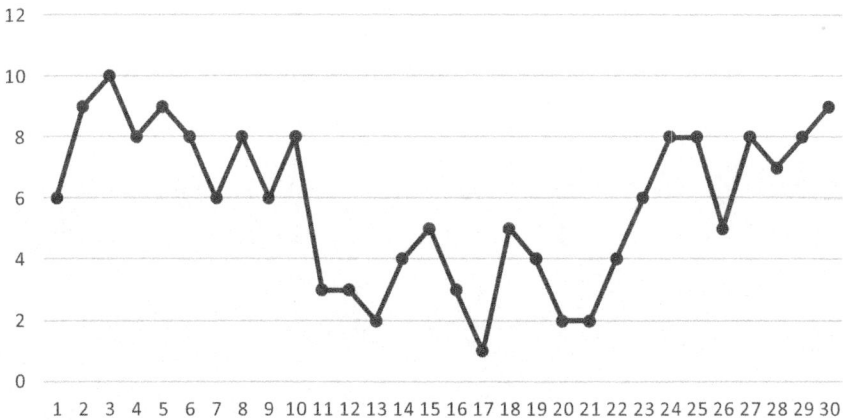

125

DECEMBER

♥ **Love** Sweeter the bells never ring ...: You will still remember this Christmas including New Year's Eve in twenty years. Venus and Mars will provide you with four weeks of non-stop love highlights - from romantic hut magic à deux to fierce smooches at Christmas parties and New Year's Eve parties. The best thing about it: Even the one-night adventure on the business trip and the secret affair with no prospect of a happy ending won't leave you with an emotional hangover.

♟ **Success** Mars moves through the sign Leo and thus in sextile to your zodiac sign. The end of the year this year can certainly be seen: You are on the winning side. The end of the year is good. You are on the winning side.

👍 **Good for** Feeling good at the end of the year

☹ **Bad for** Not being satisfied

✦ **Best star partners** Gemini, Libra, Sagittarius

Energy level Libra: December 2024

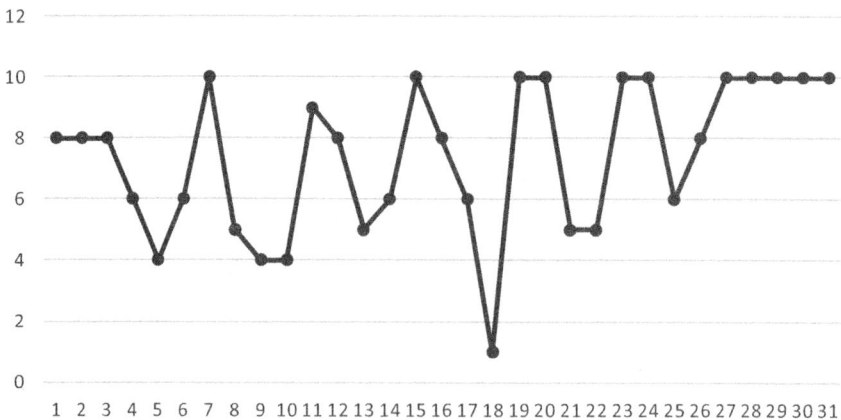

SKORPIO
(October 24-November 22)

Cosmic queen of the year 2024 is the sun. This gives your life more summer quality with all the beautiful things that a summer brings: light, beauty and love. Jupiter, the star that bears the auspicious name "planet of luck," is exactly opposite your zodiac sign until mid-May. So you will keep encountering good fortune. Uranus, a star that gives new impetus to life, stays right there throughout the year. He takes care that your life remains exciting and thrilling. And then you also get Saturn. He normally acts as a know-it-all or even a blocker, but in 2024 he will help you especially in interpersonal matters. Pluto, your personal ruler planet, has shaped your life for the last 15 years. It has not always been easy. It demands depth, thoroughness, intimacy and truth. Starting in 2024, this planet moves on and sets you free.

Of course, you also want to know what to expect in terms of health. Only good things come from the planets mentioned so far, including the Sun. You will sleep better, have more strength, be fit, stay healthy. We have to go into Pluto a little longer. This star is now in a square to your zodiac sign. Especially if your birthday is around October 24, you should do something for your health and drink a lot, eat healthy, exercise daily, purify your body with cleansing tea, get a lot of fresh air and sun. Neptune gets a wonderful task: usually this planet helps you, makes you open to the problems of life. Especially when it comes to confidence, you can rely on this star. He gives you strength when it comes to taking the right path. He is like an ally who tells you how to proceed when you have already tried everything else.

LOVE
Lucky star Jupiter occupies your partner house. This makes love enjoyable, stress-free and relaxed! You notice more and more every day that your relationships are not only about mutual obligations, but about ten-

derness, words of endearment, nice attentions and spontaneous ideas. You have sex more often and more fun doing it. Saturn gives you more personal maturity. This is especially beneficial to the singles among you, because you bring yourself in right from the start as you are, and not disguised or glossed over. This has the effect that you don't have to put things right later and thus save yourself grueling arguments. Do the stars promise a new partner? Yes, with the addition: something very special. He, or she, resembles the planet Jupiter. You meet someone who gives you the feeling of being destined as your soul mate from a higher, cosmic place. This is something very special and unique. It happens very rarely in life. It is also not so easy to describe, because in the end it is a miracle. In any case, invisible threads of energy run between your hearts, and it's as if your souls are merging.

"Cosmic power, your stars lead to success in 2024!"

CAREER

Your career is really boosted by the Sun, Jupiter and Uranus. Successes are certain, and even lots of extra work can't take away your desire to succeed. Your work will not be hard and joyless anyway. You will always have enough time in between to take a deep breath and recharge your batteries. The best thing is that Jupiter in your opposite sign provides for people who help you, promote you. In individual cases it is even possible that people invest money in you because they are absolutely convinced of your special abilities. Even if you don't work (anymore), they have a great year ahead of them. With Uranus opposite your zodiac sign, you will never feel bored. Every day you invent something new, exciting, thrilling. This may include continuing your education at community college or elsewhere. Jupiter and Uranus awaken your interest in taking up a healing or counseling profession. You may book a seminar or outright training in astrology or another spiritual subject. Some of you may also become involved in volunteer work. Your desire to help will certainly play the main role in this. Pluto also has a special role to play here: as already mentioned, it pushes for change and renewal. In individual cases, this can also mean that you hang up your previous activity. In principle, openness is the order of the day for your future. But you can be sure that this planet will only put things in front of you that are ultimately good for you.

CHARACTER:	Bold, fearless, determined
PERSONAL APPEARANCE:	Energetic, powerful, mysterious
FEELING:	Passionate, deep
STONE:	Jasper
TIER:	Panther
FLOWER:	Lotus
BEST DAY:	Tuesday

JANUARY

Now Pluto is in the zodiac sign Aquarius, where it will stay for almost 20 years. There's certainly nothing wrong with getting ready for it now: Pluto demands change. It means letting go of habits to make way for something new and better.

💜 *Love* Venus is taking its time and so is love: no exciting encounters, either with your current partner or with someone new you have met.

🏆 *Success* The Sun and Mars are in the zodiac sign of Capricorn. These are good guidelines for career success. However, Mercury is unfavorable until the middle of the month. You should not expect easy business connections there.

👍 *Good for* Connecting with people who are different from you.

☹ *Bad for* Being despondent.

✦ *Best star partners* Virgo, Capricorn

Energy level Scorpio: January 2024

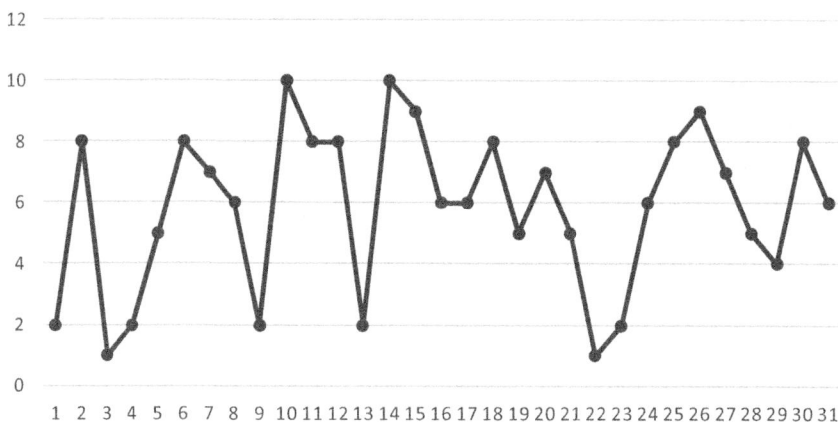

FEBRUARY

💜 **Love** You will be satisfied whether you devote yourself to the carnival or prefer to celebrate with your partner in a very intimate and private way. In the second half of the month, be sure to be mindful of each other: There's contention in the air. And there is another warning: Watch your money, be economical with it, and no acquisitions!

🏆 **Success** Assume that it will be rather uncomfortable. You must also reckon with the fact that something that you think is already in the clear is dragging on. Now you need calm blood and rush in no case to be persuaded to anything that is not one hundred percent sure.

👍 **Good for** A New Love

☹ **Bad for** Loneliness

✨ **Best star partners** Scorpio, Pisces, Capricorn

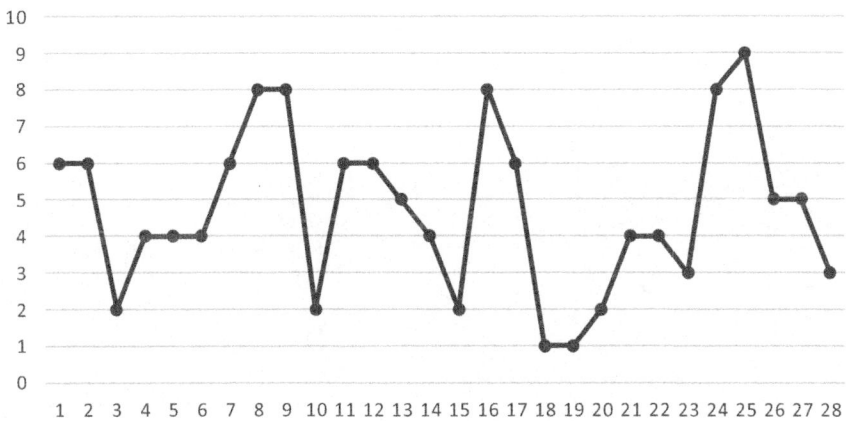

Energy level Scorpio: February 2024

MARCH

♥ **Love** Mars and Venus conjoin in the first half of the month and help you to be luckier in love. One more thing is important: You should keep your body fit, so that you can keep up with your great luck and don't get tired.

♕ **Success** In terms of success, the stars will give you a helping hand. You have one of your strongest performances in March, the most stamina and the smartest idea. That doesn't mean playing to the gallery now, either. You're a Scorpio who knows exactly when it's your time. Step on the brakes firmly again from March 20: Whoever darts further now will end up in the off.

👍 **Good for** More Influence.

☹ **Bad for** Relationships where nothing is going on.

✦ **Best star partners** Aquarius, Capricorn, Pisces, Scorpio

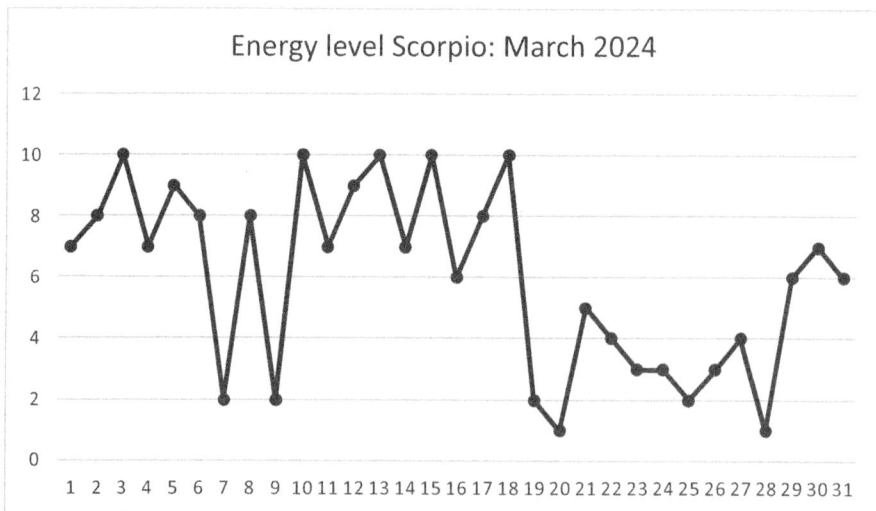

Energy level Scorpio: March 2024

132

APRIL

💜 **Love** Planet Mars awakens your lust and sensuality. Unfortunately Venus does not play along. In individual cases, this can sometimes lead to a big fight in your partner's life. Another problem you may have to deal with this month is jealousy. But there you should restrain yourself. Jealousy is not an issue for you in April.

🏆 **Success** You have good, to say you, great opportunities, but also have to make an effort. Get nothing as a gift in the first 20 days of April. But with proper effort, the stars also promise good rewards. At the end of the month, more money is also promised.

👍 **Good for** Looking for a new job.

☹ **Bad for** Not getting out of a bad job situation.

✨ **Best star partners** Capricorn, Virgo, Taurus

Energy level Scorpio: April 2024

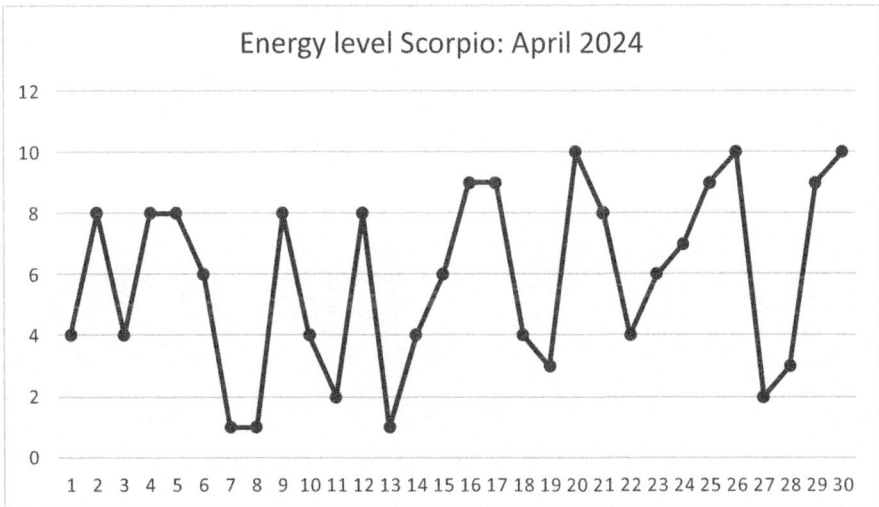

MAY

💜 *Love* In the first half of May, Jupiter and Venus are opposite your zodiac sign, opening a window into the land of love. The fact that it doesn't come to a climax after all is due to Mars and its impatience.

🏆 *Success* Uranus moves into a great position in May and opens up whole new possibilities for you: A new job? Finally, the right apartment? Everything is possible. He is even ready for more money. What you can do for this is: connect in spirit with this Uranus. Make him your friend. Greet him every morning, welcome him, make him your friend!

👍 *Good for* Wait and see and not start anything new

☹ *Bad for* A new love

✦ *Best star partners* Virgo, Capricorn, Pisces

Energy level Scorpio: May 2024

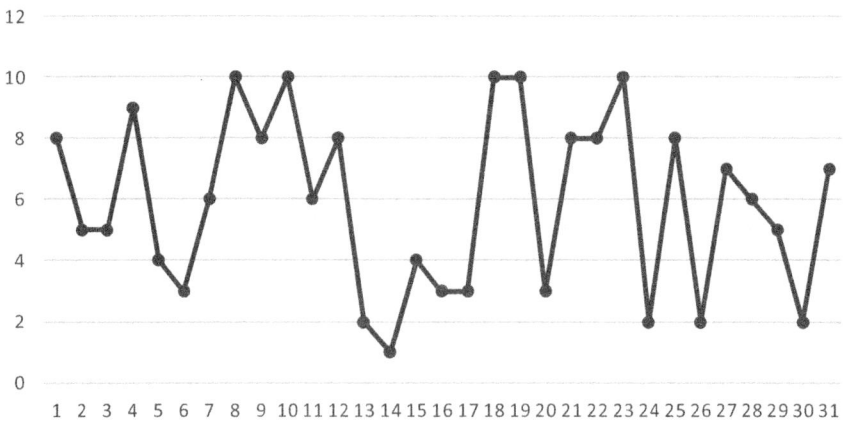

JUNE

💜 **Love** During the first week of June, there may be a cloud or two over your love prospects. But then Mars moves into your opposite sign, Taurus. If you want it even more awesome, wait until the 18th of the month. That's when Venus takes you by the hand and leads you straight into the land of love.

🏆 **Success** Uranus is opposite your sign. But he's being watched over by Saturn. I.e. that he can bring in his changes only sparingly. You can look forward to it in the fourth week of the month. There you are confronted with a task where others give up. But you outgrow yourself and create a positive result. Great!

👍 **Good for** Setting a goal and sticking to it until it is fulfilled.

☹ **Bad for** Resignation

✨ **Best star partners** Capricorn, Cancer, Taurus

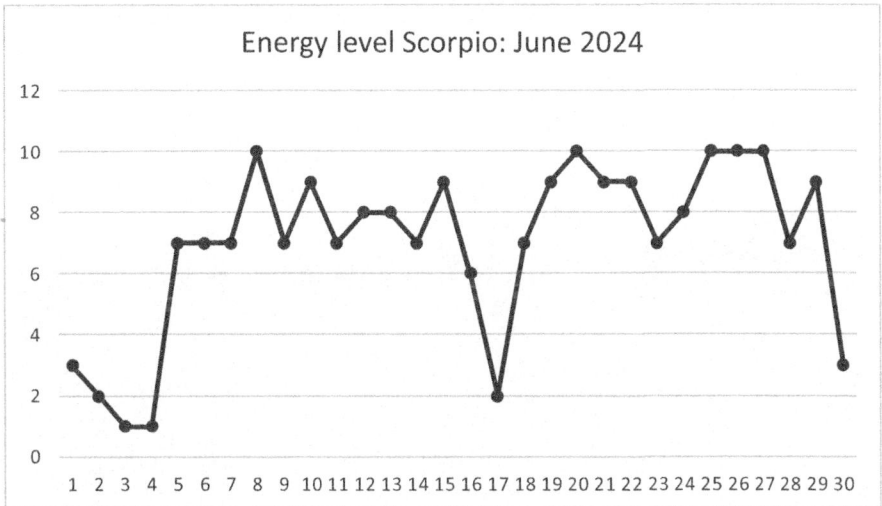

Energy level Scorpio: June 2024

JULY

❤️ **Love** Passion and sex are in your astrogram during the first week. You may also well make a firm commitment. Quite a few of you will marry and start a family. If you are already in a relationship, you will also fully enjoy the great stars and will realize: love is and remains the most beautiful and greatest force in life.

🏆 **Success** Saturn moves into a position that is decidedly important for you. This means that you can come out of yourself more and once again show what you are made of. For your job, this means raising your hand when extra work, new assignments, or anything else is given. Even if nothing comes back at the moment, you will get your deserved reward..

👍 **Good for** Strengthening friendships and making new ones.

☹️ **Bad for** Just living side by side

✦ **Best star partners** Cancer, Pisces, Scorpio

Energy level Scorpio: July 2024

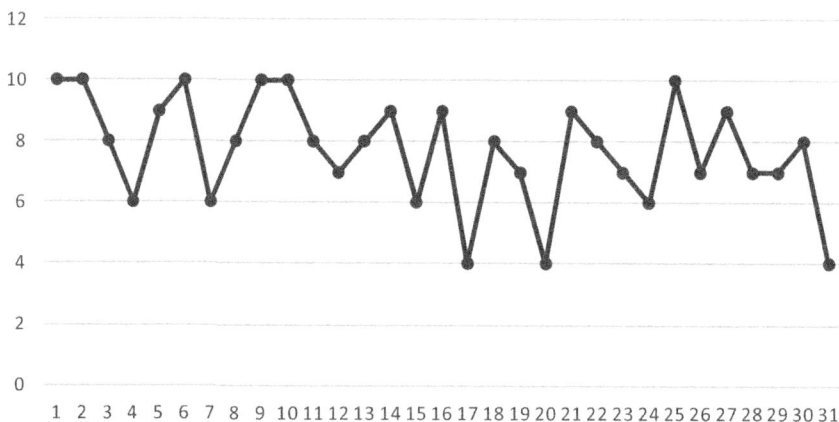

AUGUST

💜 *Love* If you're already in a relationship, you feel a new desire to make life more enjoyable for the two of you, to enjoy the days. Gone are the days of high expectations and accusations when something went differently than you planned. Singles also feed on the cosmic energies, lower the demands on the other and let themselves completely unprejudiced on the experiment love.

🏆 *Success* Neptune in the zodiac sign Pisces does not make you megalomaniac, if he puts the desire in your brain that there is still much more to achieve in your professional life. Best time for corresponding ambitions: around the full moon on the 19th and on the following days in August.

👍 *Good for* Getting ahead, making money

☹ *Bad for* Waiting for better opportunities

✦ *Best star partners* Capricorn, Virgo, Taurus

Energy level Scorpio: August 2024

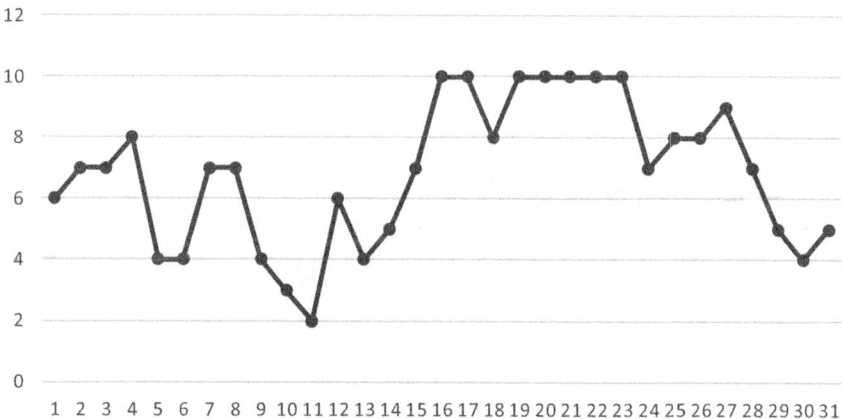

SEPTEMBER

♥ *Love* You can't help but love "totally", full of devotion and intensity. Do you always get the same in return? Mostly not - at least until now. But in September Saturn provides a balance. He changes your attitude to partnerships bit by bit. You think more about yourself and still about your partner. Singles also benefit from this change. You finally get involved in a commitment without any inhibitions. Carefree times are coming your way.

🏆 *Success* You are appreciated, and that builds you up! But you are also needed: In September, you can make it big, succeed, move up, make money, even reap fame, but you also need to believe in yourself. Have more confidence in yourself and don't always push yourself into the background!

👍 *Good for* Taking care of your health

☹ *Bad for* Just letting things go

✦ *Best star partners* Virgo

Energy level Scorpio: September 2024

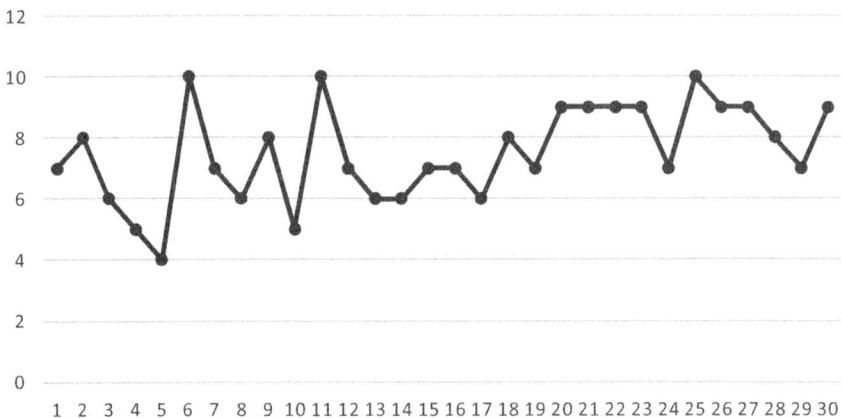

138

OCTOBER

💜 **Love** Venus is in your zodiac sign and Mars is in Cancer. This promises days (and nights) of lust and love, exciting togetherness, flirtations, and even chances for a lifelong partnership. There are even additional hints coming from heaven: If you are a woman, then you should quietly hide a bit and even pretend that you are not interested in love at all. Men however get the request to confess completely openly to the love.

🏆 **Success** Strong stars for the freelancers: There are chances for new contacts, new markets and new partnership shoulder. Basically be careful in October, and postpone important decisions!

👍 **Good for** Taking time as it is.

☹ **Bad for** Being suspicious

✨ **Best star partners** Taurus, Virgo, Pisces

Energy level Scorpio: October 2024

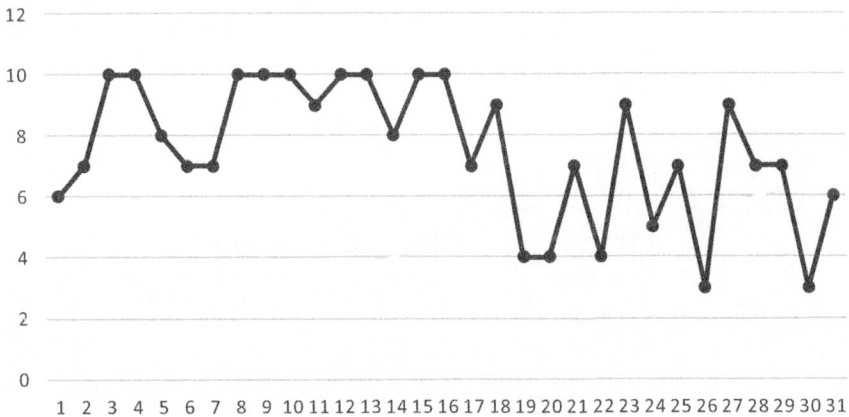

NOVEMBER

💜 **Love** If love didn't exist, the beginning of the month would be a real runaway. But the stars comfort you, and you laugh a lot, flirt, flirt, love. Then, in the second half of the month, planet Venus takes a good position in the zodiac sign Capricorn. This also helps you to sort out any problems.

🏆 **Success** The positive influences predominate in November. But there are also problems. Right at the beginning of the month, around the New Moon, you are served a difficult task. Do your best! But: Don't worry! Self-reproaches are really superfluous; you don't have to blame yourself if things go wrong!

👍 **Good for** Positive experiences in love

☹ **Bad for** Just keep doing what you're doing

✨ **Best star partners** Pisces, Aquarius, Sagittarius

Energy level Scorpio: November 2024

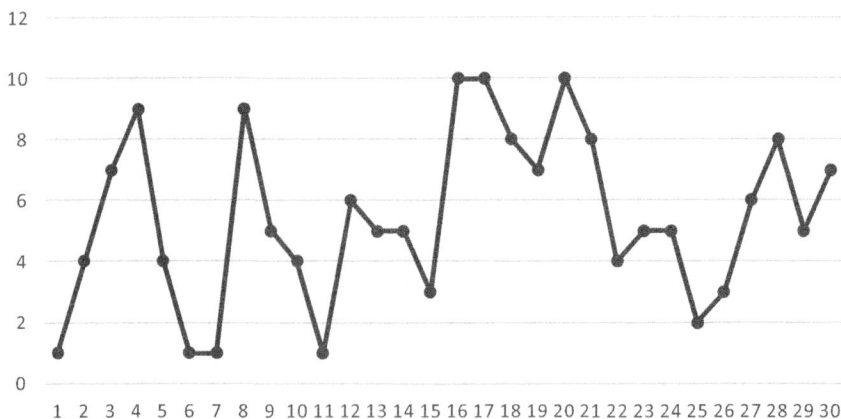

DECEMBER

💜 *Love* The love star Venus smiles at you for the next four weeks. It is clear that you dream of exciting encounters, love and eroticism. But your very real life also comes under the spell of this star. Others are interested in you, and you may meet someone who likes you and who also likes you.

🏆 *Success* At work, your commitment counts. Unfortunately, things don't go your way either; others call the shots and talk over you. Only in the last week of December you get the liberating feeling that you are in charge of your own life. To confirm this, you also have a great sense of achievement. Even more money is possible.

👍 *Good for* Friendships

☹ *Bad for* Trivialities and side issues

✦ *Best star partners* Cancer, Capricorn, Scorpio, Pisces

Energy level Scorpio: December 2024

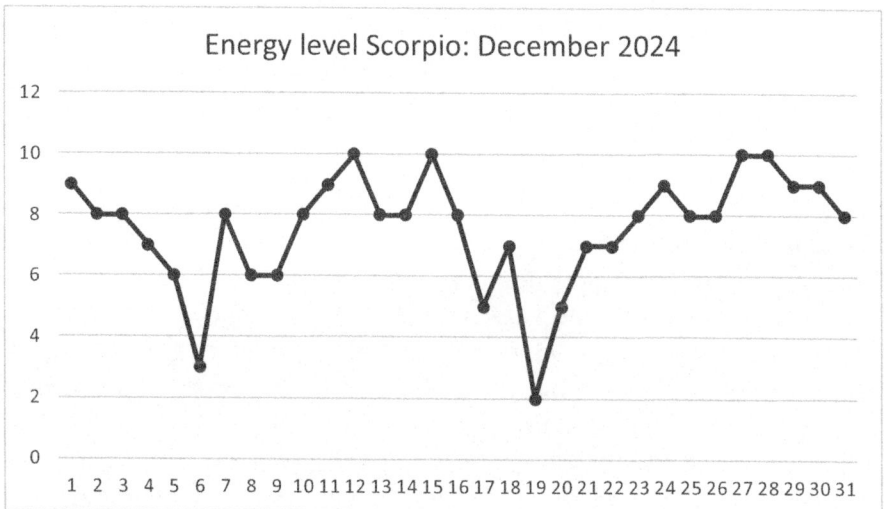

SAGITTARIUS
(November 23-December 21)

The year 2024 is ruled by the Sun. This is already a great advantage, because there are great similarities between your zodiac sign and the Sun. This may surprise you now, because the Sun belongs to the summer, but you are a winter sign. But that is only one side. Similarity consists in the fact that you both "radiate ", the sun outward, you inward. Your warmth comes from giving meaning. Another huge plus is that Jupiter is exactly opposite your zodiac sign from May 25. He is your personal ruling planet, and this complements what was said before, namely that you spread warmth, because nothing fills us humans as much as happiness. You get another boost from Pluto. This planet did not play an important role for you in the last 15 years. But now he is in the sign of Aquarius, forming a sextile to your zodiac sign. Now you receive its special power. It consists in understanding life from a higher point of view, that is, always the superior and whole. This planet is also very similar to your Jupiter in that immediate benefits do not count for it. With this Pluto in Aquarius, you become a visionary. You feel deeply what the world needs, what it lacks, and you will see to it that it is fulfilled in small and large things. All together, for you, a Sagittarius, it is as if you are in a chariot of triumph, being pulled by horses to where our world needs happiness. Dag provides you with great opportunities to realize yourself and be happy and content yourself.

LOVE
Naturally, your stars in love make for a great year. Astrology claims that the Sun's reign causes you yourself to shine more, be friendlier and happier, and, this is something very special, really captivate other people. A particularly magical time window opens at the beginning of spring on March 21, 2024. The Sun now comes closer to you every day, and with Jupiter, from May 25 you almost have something like a guarantee: you will meet the, or the "divine" lover, who has everything you dream of. If you are already in a steady partnership, you will rediscover how perfect

this love is. What you need to know is that Pluto is also involved in the subject of love. This looks like, for example, that you no longer want to put up with inadequacies in your own relationship. You will try to change it by talking, but you ARE also ready to take the final step and separate. If Jupiter is exactly opposite your zodiac sign in the second half of the year, you will also have no problem at all finding a new partner, one who is more in line with your ideas of love. With people who interest you, even if you are still in a committed relationship, you have to reckon from July 2024 in any case. Then it depends entirely on you what happens.

Sun and Jupiter 2024:
Radiant luck in the chariot of triumph

CAREER

Credibility, competence and charisma are the qualities with which you make a great impression in the solar year and achieve corresponding success. During the first four months, you will also need a critical eye at times. You are too trusting and naive. Therefore, do not decide anything without thorough examination and always consult an expert for important contracts. From May 25 you can count on Jupiter. You will be accurate, reliable and make great impression. Let's move on to Pluto. This celestial body has been next to your zodiac sign in Capricorn for the past fifteen years. It obscured your view of the sky. Now it has moved one sign further and opens a window into infinity. This is good for you, giving you optimism and a belief in security and peace. Your personal life benefits from it. It is most definitely also the case that this Pluto gives you the power to live and spread your visions of a better world.

CHARACTER:	Jovial, helpful, benevolent
PERSONAL APPEARANCE:	Relaxed, serene, infectious
FEELING:	Enthusiastic
STONE:	Lapis lazuli
ANIMAL:	Horse
PLANT:	Pine
BEST DAY:	Thursday

JANUARY

♥ *Love* With Mars in in the zodiac sign of Capricorn, you are feeling your best. Especially when you hear about the relationship crises around you. Will it come to a partnership? Fine! If not: inshallah! Planet Venus makes you strong in your partnership. You take care of yourself, treat yourself well, and no longer define your happiness exclusively in terms of harmony.

♕ *Success* You present yourself as a whole more courageous and direct in January. Especially those who want to apply for a job, change jobs or start their own business will benefit from this. However, the stars also take care of those who have been loyal to a company for many years. You also get a kick and can suddenly improve, change, stimulate something at your workplace. People listen to you, implement your ideas.

👍 *Good for* Self-discipline, self-control

☹ *Bad for* Arrogance, complacency

✦ *Best star partners* Aquarius, Leo

Energy level Sagittarius: January 2024

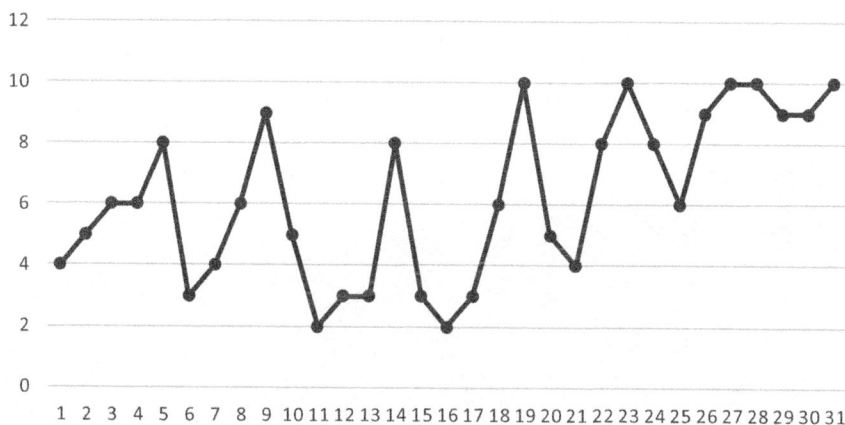

FEBRUARY

Now Pluto is in the astrological sign Aquarius, where it will stay for almost 20 years. So it is certainly not wrong to get ready for it now: Pluto demands change. It means letting go of habits to make way for something new and better.

💜 *Love* Congratulations! Mars and Venus embrace from the middle of the month. This is meant to be a default. In other words, do the same with your partner, make time for love!

🏆 *Success* The second half of the month is definitely better than the first. There you can even count on a profit. However, if possible, do not make important agreements in the second half of the month.

👍 *Good for* Positive attitude towards life

☹ *Bad for* Relationships that are not really right anyway

✨ *Best star partners* Leo, Virgo and Capricorn

Energy level Sagittarius: February 2024

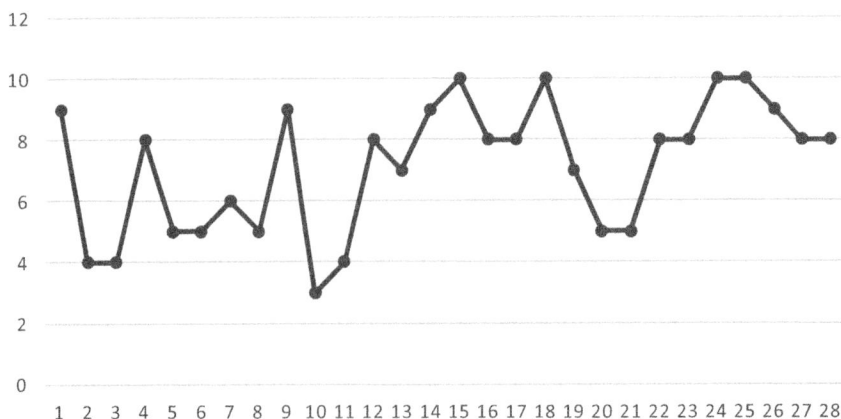

MARCH

💜 *Love* For you, spring begins this year already on March 1. Mars and Venus are in the zodiac sign Aquarius. Saturn, in turn, takes care that you meet exactly the people who suit you. If you are already in a relationship, you will not forget this special beginning of spring for a long time.

🏆 *Success* March offers you good opportunities. Sure, they don't just fall from the sky. They need all your strength. But after all, you're a Sagittarius who gets really strong when challenged. That is the case now. Go for it! Do your best! It looks quite that you may enjoy a great sense of achievement, may also have to do with more money.

👍 *Good for* Courage

☹ *Bad for* Do nothing to find happiness

✦ *Best star partners* Aquarius

Energy level Sagittarius: March 2024

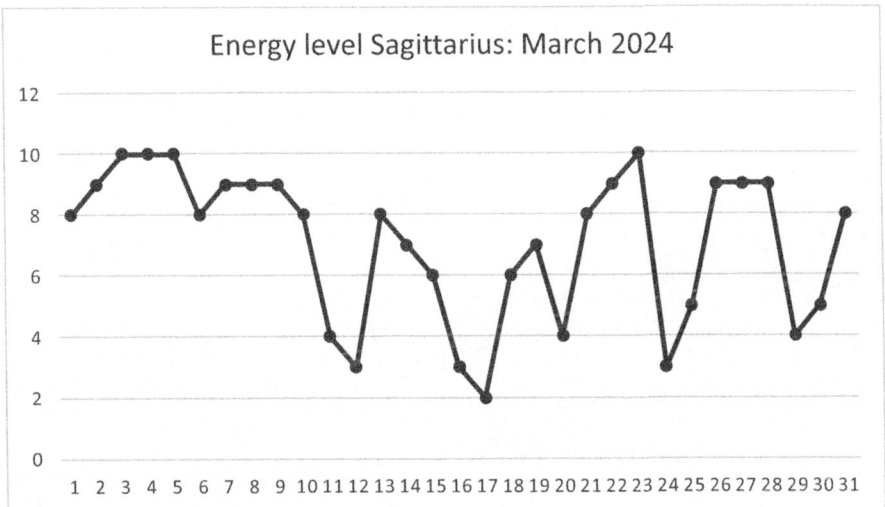

APRIL

💜 **Love** You are doing well in April. But our world is not only made up of people who are generous. Everyone thinks only of themselves, and when you come along and show how well you are doing, others are seized with jealousy. So keep a low profile and, more importantly, spread your luck.

🏆 **Success** You have good stars in April and can accomplish a lot. However, the stars also think that you should not only think about yourself now, but about the world as a whole. You have something to give, and that's what matters now. You can do it. What you also need to know is that around the 20th of the month is a time for you where you experience something important.

👍 **Good for** Success, enjoy life

☹ **Bad for** Dissatisfaction

✦ **Best star partners** Aquarius, Gemini

Energy level Sagittarius: April 2024

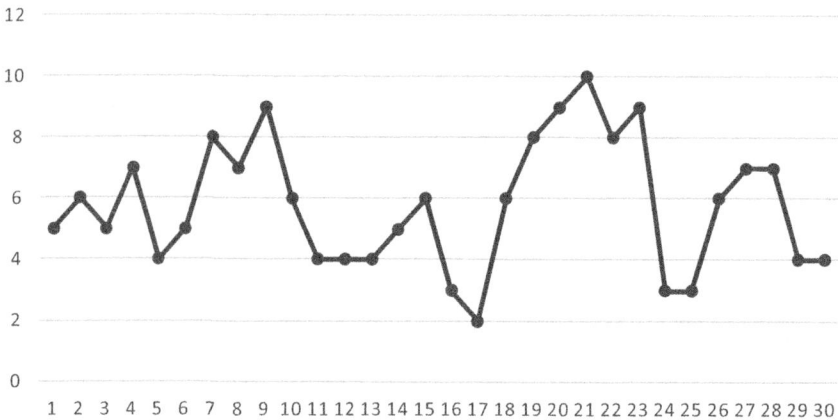

MAY

💜 *Love* Planet Mars is doing you good. It is in Aries, a fire sign like yours, Sagittarius. Therefore, assume that you have an optimal companion, a spirit that will stand by you. At the end of May you will also receive confirmation. You succeed in something that you yourself no longer believed in. You experience a great experience in love.

🏆 *Success* Jupiter soon enters a new sign, namely Gemini. Then he will be exactly opposite your sign. This will allow you to create something that you, your family and everyone you know will be proud of. Start thinking now about what can really enrich your life.

👍 *Good for* General advancement

☹ *Bad for* Getting stuck on one problem for too long

✨ *Best star partners* Aries, Libra

Energy level Sagittarius: May 2024

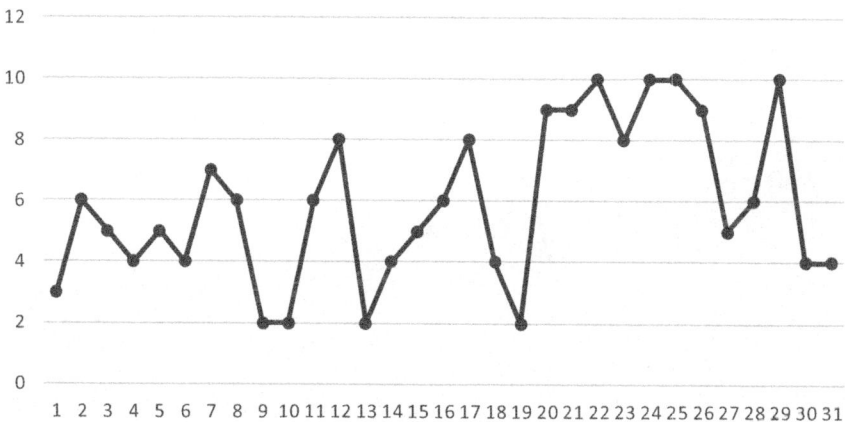

JUNE

💜 **Love** Jupiter carries the epithet lucky planet. It has taken up residence opposite your zodiac sign. This makes you an interesting, loving, generous partner. If you are living alone right now, you should be very open, because there is a good chance that you will meet the person who is meant for you. So you can expect an increase in partnerships and even marriages in the Sagittarius camp.

🏆 **Success** You enjoy a stable high in June: no stress, no hectic, no competitive pressure. Everything speaks for you to discover new sources of money and to use them. No peak is too high for you, no problem too tricky, no hurdle too insurmountable. Nevertheless, you would do well to follow your instincts. Especially in the last week of June you are extremely sensitive.

👍 **Good for** Success, money

☹ **Bad for** Ingratitude

✦ **Best star partners** Sagittarius, Gemini, Aries

Energy level Sagittarius: June 2024

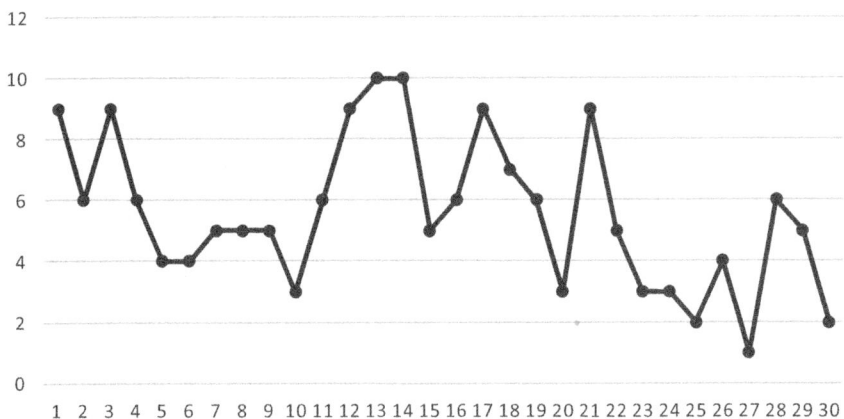

JULY

💜 *Love* You have great stars in July. which also benefit your love life. Now you meet the one, or the right one, a person who is interested not only in your body but also in your soul. You have been waiting for this being for a long time. Your current partner will fade into the background a bit. But that doesn't mean you're breaking up with him.

🏆 *Success* The Sun moves through the zodiac sign Cancer until the 20th of the month. You should be properly attuned to this, and it means that you are not too theoretical, that is, "cerebral". You do better business, for example, if you show your feelings or at least make them known.

👍 *Good for* Naturality

☹ *Bad for* Not believing in yourself

✨ *Best star partners* Sagittarius, Gemini, Aries

Energy level Sagittarius: July 2024

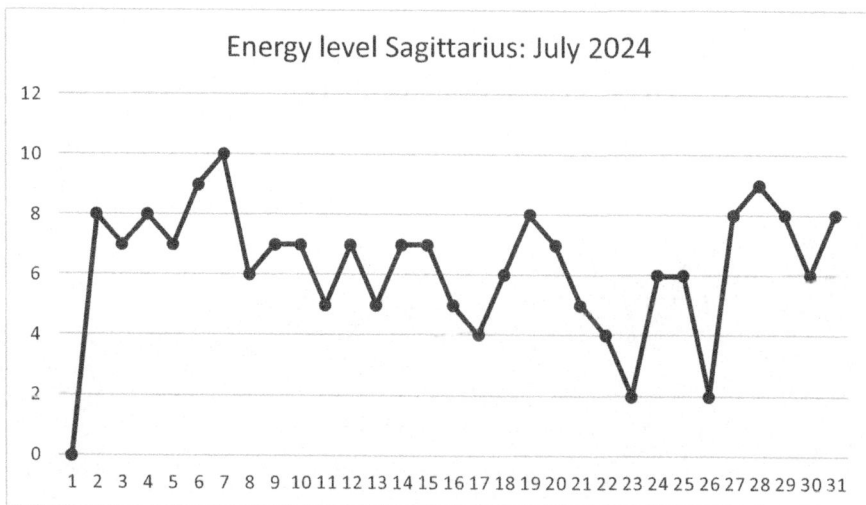

AUGUST

♥ *Love* The Sun as the regent of the new year awakens your best sides - and now, in August especially: contentment, happiness and capacity for love. You love with more devotion because you can't help it, but you don't demand anything in return. Marriages blossom again because your tolerance is appreciated. Singles also get to know someone much more often because you no longer chase ideals, but give everyone a chance who makes an effort for you. And the greatest thing: More desire comes through the sun. You'll feel this especially in bed, even after many, many years of marriage.

♕ *Success* With Mars and Jupiter opposite your zodiac sign, you'll blossom, grow and develop in August. Your talents will take hold. You will also benefit from the network you have created. People approach you with tailored offers in their pockets.

👍 *Good for* Love and Tenderness

☹ *Bad for* Competition, Rival

✦ *Best star partners* Leo, Gemini

Energy level Sagittarius: August 2024

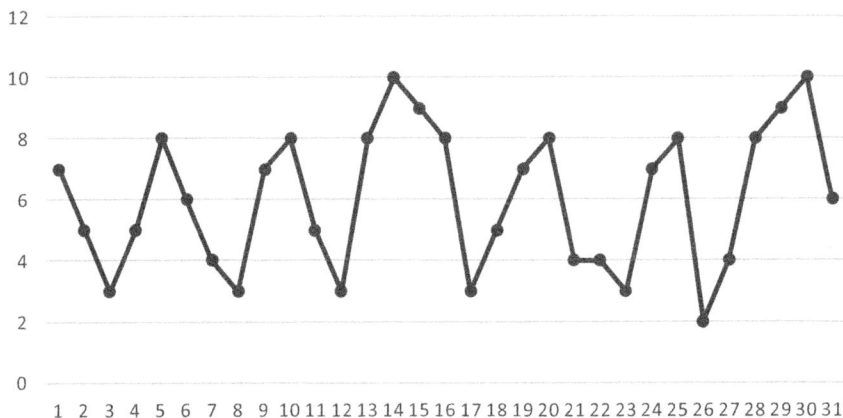

SEPTEMBER

💜 **Love** You have the planet Jupiter to thank for your confidence in September: Why be jealous? There's no one better than you anyway, so there's no reason to cheat on you. Singles

🏆 **Success** No goal too high and no wish too unrealistic: Your astrological calendar reveals dazzling times with fantastic conditions to achieve above average things. Too bad, around the new moon - it takes place on September 3 - you get into brooding. The right therapy? Anything that distracts from dull thoughts. There is no real reason to worry. At the end of the month you are quite intolerant.

👍 **Good for** Contentment

☹ **Bad for** Quarrels and arguments

✨ **Best star partners** Leo, Gemini

Energy level Sagittarius: September 2024

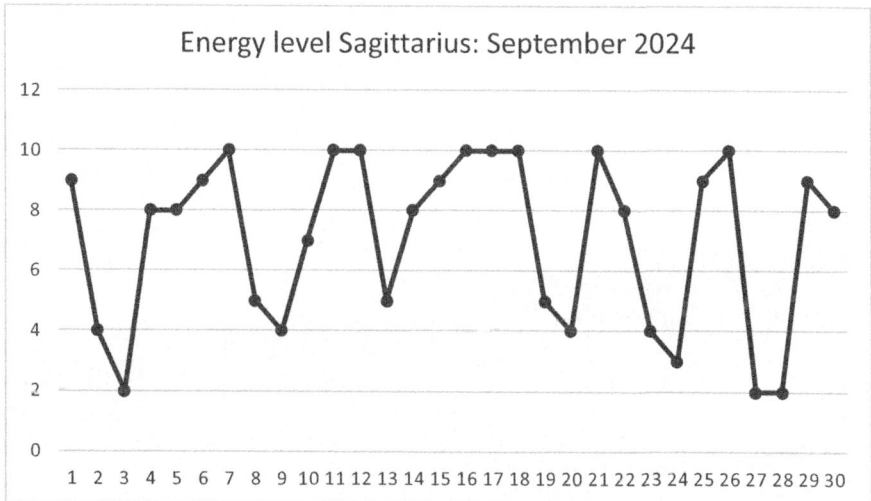

OCTOBER

💜 **Love** You'd be well advised to use your head and distrust your feelings in October. Don't worry, it's not a big story, but if you keep this in mind, it will get easier. Towards the end of the month things will be right again in love. In individual cases, this could also include walking down the aisle with your partner.

🏆 **Success** In October, there will be nothing about casually twiddling your thumbs. Your career demands everything. Keep up with it, then you can laugh at the end! There is one extra hint: The stars indicate that you cannot rely on friends unconditionally in October. So please no agreements that are not one hundred percent sure!

👍 **Good for** Momentum, power, assert yourself and win

☹ **Bad for** Becoming immoderate

✦ **Best star partners** Aries, Sagittarius, Leo

Energy level Sagittarius: October 2024

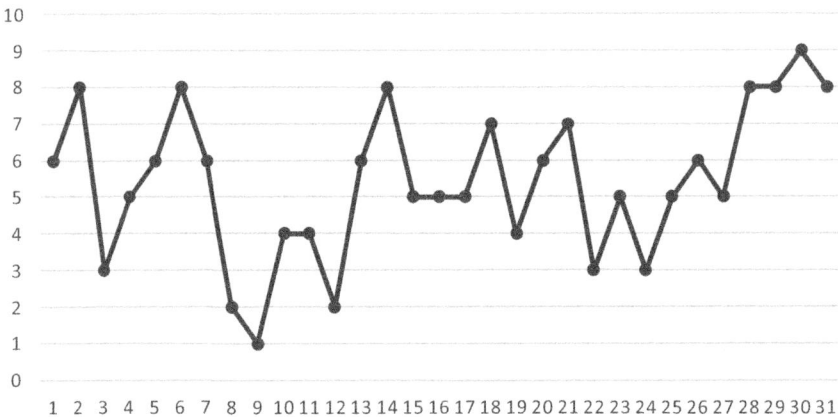

NOVEMBER

♥ **Love** Love is beautiful and goes to the heart. Only around the New Moon on November 1 may world-weariness arise. But from the 10th of the month you are almost in love heaven thanks to a strong planet Mars. However, you do not believe this yourself at first, because a difficulty appears. But at the latest from the 10th of the month you can be quite sure.

♆ **Success** The bad news first: Your job will be exhausting, because in November you have to tactic, weigh, court, give in, and that is unusual for an optimistically thinking Sagittarius. On top of that, you miss your power until the 10th of the month, get tired quickly and feel the new moon right at the beginning of November. The good news is: after the 20th everything will be great.

👍 **Good for** Slow down and concentrate. Don't rush things.

☹ **Bad for** Taking care of yourself

✦ **Best star partners** Leo, Libra

Energy level Sagittarius: November 2024

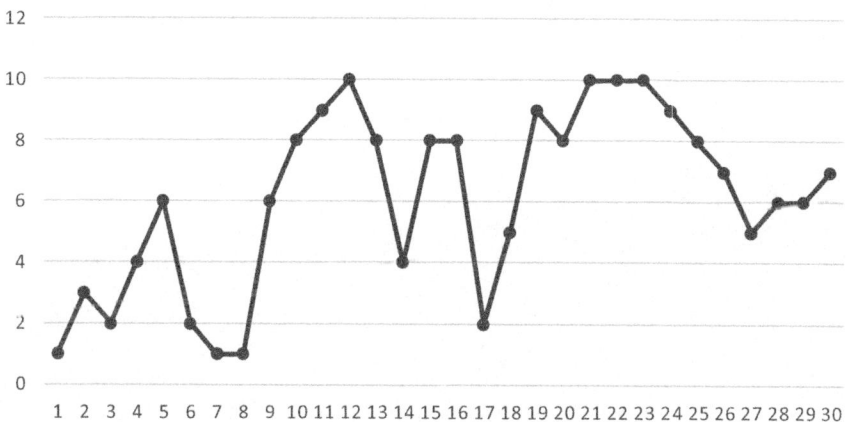

DECEMBER

💜 **Love** The Sun in your zodiac sign conjures up a great vibe for you, and you find plenty of time for your lover. If you're solo, the second half of the month could even bring a delightful encounter that you'll still be celebrating twenty years from now.

🏆 **Success** With the exception of a few days, Fortuna takes you to task for three weeks. You are in top form, show yourself to be in a good mood and cut a fabulous fi-gure. These are also the best pre-requisites for business: You have a fabulous talent for selling yourself well. From the 20th, just in time for Christmas, things will be quieter.

👍 **Good for** Luck, success, money

☹ **Bad for** Displeasure, bad moods

✦ **Best star partners** Sagittarius, Libra, Aquarius, Gemini

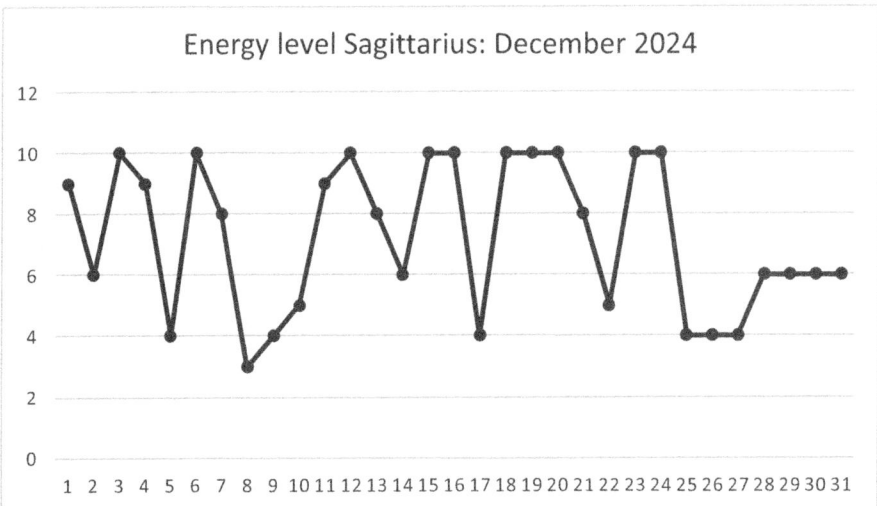

Energy level Sagittarius: December 2024

CAPRICORN
(December 22-January 20)

The Sun is the regent of the year 2024. Under guarantee you will experience more light than shadow and happily encounter the lightness of being. Through the power of the Sun, your personal ruler planet Saturn also gets a much more positive face. The last two and a half years he moved through the sign Aquarius. This caused changes, small ones that you often didn't even notice and big ones that may still be bothering you today. In any case, your life lacked what is actually considered typical for your zodiac sign, namely stability. For the next two and a half years your Saturn will be in the zodiac sign of Pisces. This has a positive and a negative effect. Negative is due to the element of Pisces. It is water, and like actual water, anything that can't swim sinks, gets lost. On the other hand, what is able to cope in water, wins, becomes better, more successful and consistent. Water-suited activities have to do with human abilities, when feelings play a role or interpersonal contact is important. Unsuitable for water, on the other hand, are activities that can also be performed by machines and computers. Absolutely suitable for water is metaphysical work. This includes helping another person, giving advice so that his life becomes easier. However, meditation and the occupation with metaphysical methods such as astrology or Tarot stand in the first place. A special effect also goes out from the fact that Pluto is no longer in your star sign in 2024, but one sign further in Aquarius. In all areas it will make things easier. Your love will be more beautiful, you will have more success in your job, everyday life will be fun and your life will lose its heaviness.

LOVE
In the interpersonal sphere, the departure of Pluto and Saturn becomes even more obvious. For here it comes to bear that you shape your love yourself. You can live a dream relationship in 2024 and be happy - you only need to imagine it exactly and in detail. Keep reminding yourself:

you are the director of your life. If you are currently single and longing for a partner, this "technique" applies especially: the more often you tell yourself that you are a wonderful person, the more often you will get confirmation from others. Then what you didn't think possible happens and you meet someone who fascinates you madly and you fall in love with each other. Everything speaks for a sensual spring, a dream summer with a dream partner.

Sun shines, luck embraces -
Success in harmony

CAREER

That planet Pluto leaves you sets in motion a process that multiplies itself independently. In other words, you are now actually ready for the way up, for more success and more money. Morse your wishes to the sky - it will fulfill them for you. Even if you are no longer employed, you will fully enjoy your great stars. Be sure to take a long trip to your dreamland for the fall. You'll feel like you're in paradise. Jupiter moves through Taurus until the end of May. This sign has always been associated with wealth, profit, gifts and favorable loans. While there is no guarantee of hitting the jackpot, you may be one of the very lucky ones. Certainly Jupiter brings peace into your life, and the sign Taurus comes over your life like a spring rain. Everything grows, is right, is accomplished, creates satisfaction. As long as Jupiter is in the zodiac sign Taurus, Uranus, which also lingers in this section, can also make itself felt much more strongly. Now you can also move and even change your profession. Change is now no longer a matter that robs you of sleep, but one that you actually welcome. As long as Jupiter is in Taurus, you will definitely not want for anything. On May 25, this Jupiter changes signs and enters Gemini. Now you will get into the swing of things. You could say you become young again, adventurous and open-minded towards life.

CHARACTER:	Serious, reliable, ambitious
PERSONAL APPEARANCE:	Reserved, disciplined
FEELING:	Controlled, loyal
STONE:	Precious Onyx
ANIMAL:	Camel
PLANT:	Cactus
BEST DAY:	Saturday

JANUARY

💜 **Love** Through Mars in Capricorn you will feel deep happiness when you have mastered a situation together with your partner. Even the singles now instinctively choose those people who are not so easy to crack and act. Why? Because it is exciting to conquer this person. For the end of the month, a particularly promising encounter is in your astro program.

🏆 **Success** Mars in Capricorn awakens a longing for apprecia-tion. If you get a lot of it, money becomes a secondary matter. Dissatisfied Capricorns should look for tasks that are sustainable, that end in a result. You need that to measure yourself. Only when you can see what you have achieved, you are satisfied.

👍 **Good for** Good performance

☹ **Bad for** Indifference

✦ **Best star partners** Capricorn, Virgo, Taurus

Energy level Capricorn: January 2024

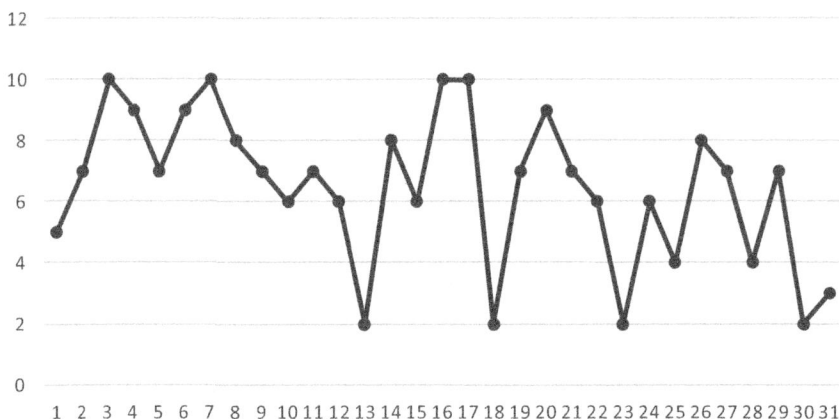

FEBRUARY

💜 **Love** Mars and Venus promise amusement. This doesn't have to be a passionate love story, but be open to merriment and love. The second half of the month will be quieter. Now work comes first anyway.

🏆 **Success** Saturn and Neptune are in the sign of Pisces. First of all, routine is required there. This also means that you should not get in-volved in anything that is not air-tight. On the other hand, the stars could also come up with a surpri-se. However, this presupposes that you do not commit yourself, but are open to the ideas of life. Miracles are only possible if you are open to them.

👍 **Good for** Being open

☹ **Bad for** The everything

✦ **Best star partners** Cancer

Energy level Capricorn: February 2024

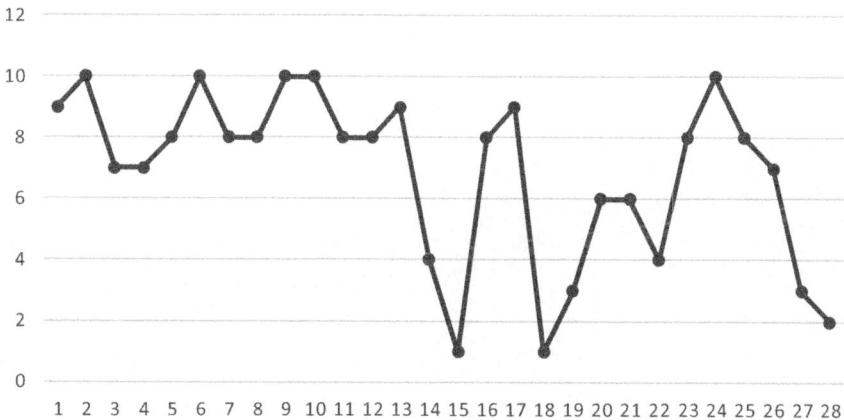

MARCH

♥ **Love** Venus is super until March 12 and gets along very well with other stars. This gives you a free ride in love. Especially for singles the chances are great. Especially around the full moon on March 25, there is a huge surprise in your stars.

♕ **Success** The Sun gives you a lot of power in March, awakens a sense of power and reveals ways to get it. You will definitely not be in the same place at the end of the month as you are today, but higher up. You will probably also earn more money or enjoy another surprise.

👍 **Good for** Love and passion

☹ **Bad for** Pessimism

✦ **Best star partners** Cancer, Scorpio

Energy level Capricorn: March 2024

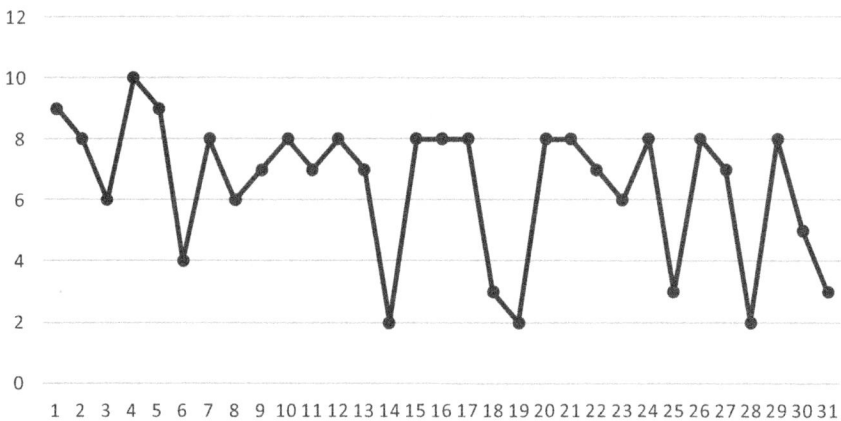

APRIL

💜 **Love** Mars and Saturn are on your side. This gives you mysterious power. With it you can seduce others, really bind them to you. You don't even have to be very active. So be careful when dealing with other people!

🏆 **Success** Your prospects for a successful professional life are more than average. What you need to know is that Saturn is in the zodiac sign of Pisces and is conjunct Venus. This calls for straightforwardness and honesty. But these are cardinal virtues of a Capricorn anyway. Your stars are especially promising on April 24. Show what you can do now, and please don't be modest!

👍 **Good for** Honesty

☹ **Bad for** Inaccuracy

✦ **Best star partners** Virgo, Capricorn, Scorpio

Energy level Capricorn: April 2024

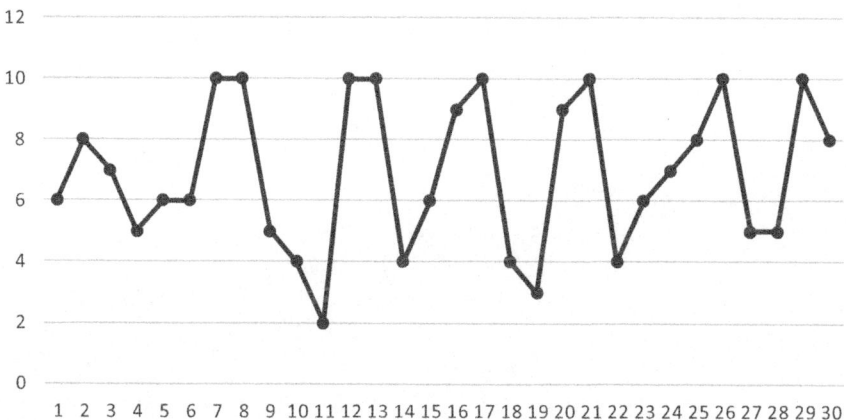

163

MAY

💜 **Love** This month and a bit of luck will bring you what you've always longed for. Maybe you are still missing the person by your side with whom life goes better. Whatever it is, assume that the stars will grant you your wish now. Just do not be immoderate right away, because Saturn is strong and fulfills only those wishes that you really deserve.

🏆 **Success** The ruler of the year, the Sun together with Jupiter, Venus, Uranus and Mercury are at your service. In other words, you have fabulous prospects. You should also really set your mind on something big and important. Now you can be proactive, bring in something new, show yourself and claim: it will succeed.

👍 **Good for** Joy and happiness

🙁 **Bad for** Doubt and seeing black

✦ **Best star partners** Cancer, Pisces

Energy level Capricorn: May 2024

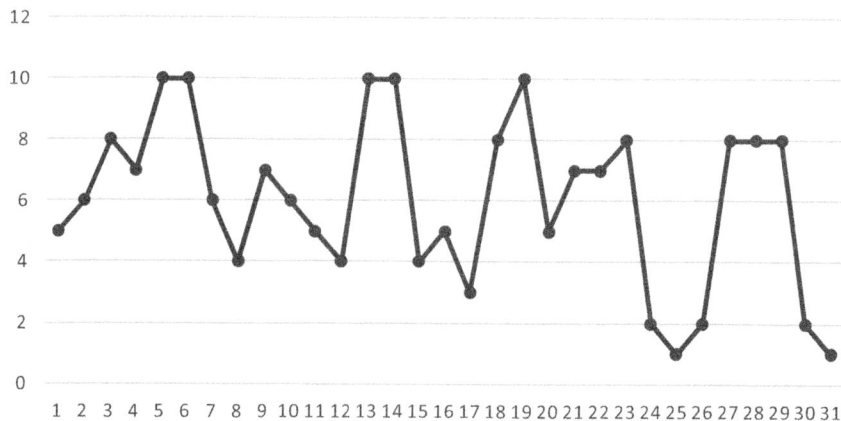

JUNE

♥ **Love** On June 10, Mars moves into a favorable position. This triggers a huge desire for love in you. If you are lucky, you will experience a great love story. If you're unlucky, you'll have to wait until the 18th of the month. There Venus takes you by the hand and leads you directly into the land of love.

♔ **Success** Uranus is in the sign of Taurus and thus in a friendly trine to your zodiac sign. Saturn and Neptune in turn form a sextile. Life is in a good mood, which can be understood as an invitation to work less or, even better, to go on vacation. From the 20th on, the cosmic situation changes, and now you can also move ahead briskly again professionally.

👍 **Good for** Joy

☹ **Bad for** Pessimism

✦ **Best star partners** Capricorn, Virgo

Energy level Capricorn: June 2024

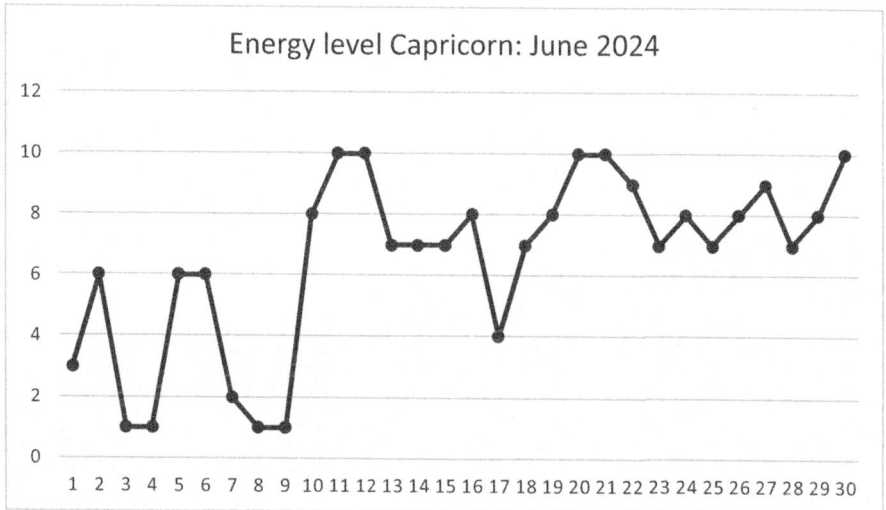

JULY

💜 *Love* The Sun is in the zodiac sign Cancer in the first three weeks of July and spreads feeling. Do you have some of that too? It's like this: You are known to be rather cool, covered, cautious on the outside. Your motto: Not everyone should immediately recognize your feelings and possibly play with them! But there are these great feelings in you. Now, in July, they are especially strong. It is quite possible that you will have a beautiful experience.

🏆 *Success* The Sun ruled the year, and now it takes position in the zodiac sign in Cancer. This can also help you professionally. Namely, you are now automatically more friendly, or simply put, a pleasant person. Especially if you work in sales, this goes down great.

👍 *Good for* Openness

☹ *Bad for* Hiding

✦ *Best star partners* Cancer, Scorpio

Energy level Capricorn: July 2024

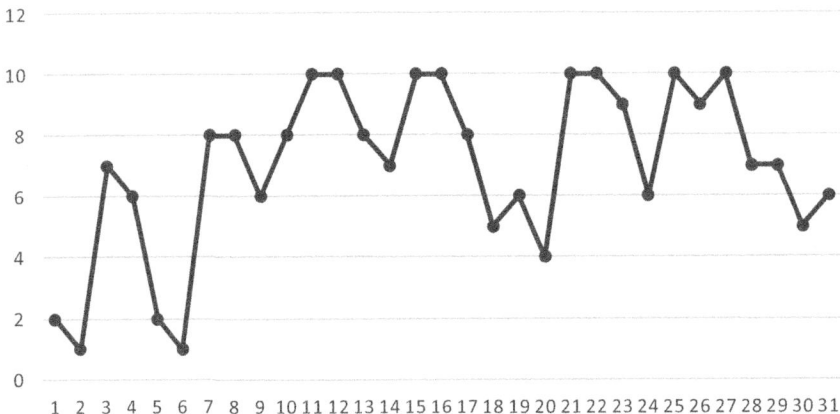

AUGUST

💜 **Love** People are crazy about you in August - especially if you're single. The reason: your ruler planet Saturn is in the sign of Pisces, conjunct the love planet Venus in Virgo. Couples take more liberties with themselves, but also concede them to their partner. And in the second half of the month the stars announce the meeting with a person who corresponds to your ideal image.

🏆 **Success** September has always been a good month for professional advancement. Feel free to let Neptune in the zodiac sign of Pisces lead you into areas that are still unknown to you.

👍 **Good for** Love

☹ **Bad for** Staying alone

✦ **Best star partners** Virgo, Capricorn

Energy level Capricorn: August 2024

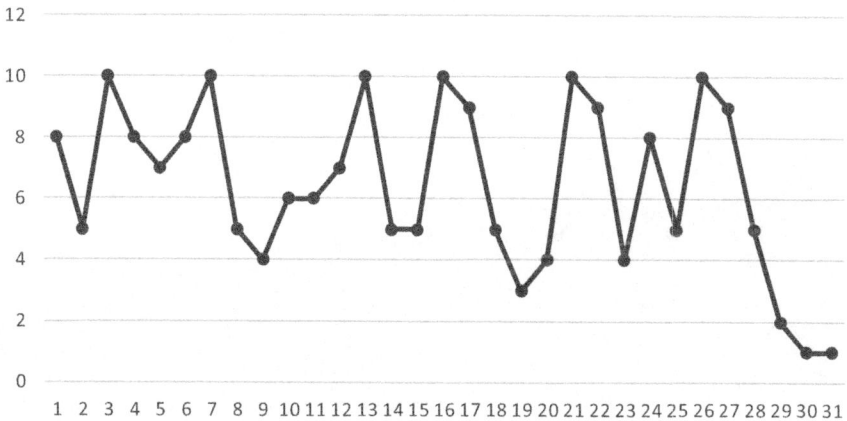

SEPTEMBER

💜 *Love* In September you are a virtuoso in the interplay of closeness and distance. Whereby you are extremely fair: What you are allowed to do, the other person is also allowed to do. Result? The relationship becomes more stable, more mature, more solid. You have found your patent remedy. Whatever is important to you moves forward: unsolved problems are taken care of, tensions are eliminated and obstacles are removed. You just have to believe in it. Thoughts sometimes work wonders.

🏆 *Success* In September you become more self-confident and at the same time calm. Setbacks? Mistakes? You can change all that. On top of that, work is really fun again because you get involved in the team and see colleagues as friends. One for all, all for one!

👍 *Good for* Optimism

☹ *Bad for* Doubting life

✦ *Best star partners* Taurus

Energy level Capricorn: September 2024

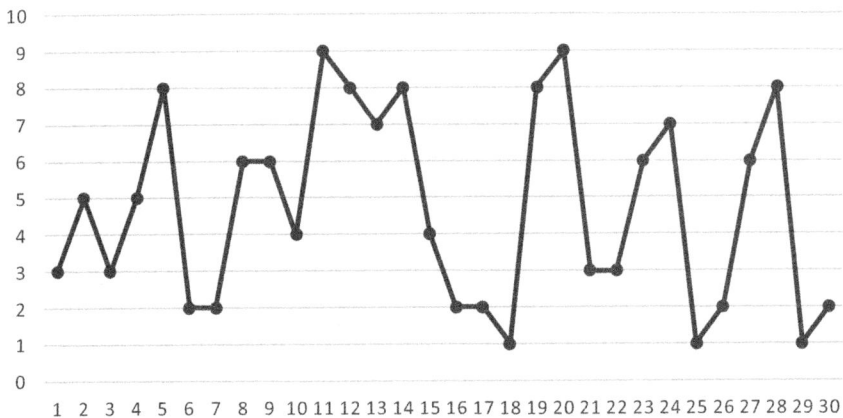

OCTOBER

💜 *Love* The love planets Venus and Mars focus completely on you in October. The probability of falling in love is thus huge - however, it remains open whether with your old partner or a new one. In any case, be ready for a surprise around the full moon on October 18!

🏆 *Success* In October you can work like a horse. Use your power; for business there are meaningful dates in your horoscope! How suc-cessful you are in the end, however, also depends on your negotiating skills. Neither with rigid perseverance nor with exaggerated compliance you make the stab. Go the way exactly in the middle!

👍 *Good for* A new love

☹ *Bad for* Discouragement

✦ *Best star partners* Taurus, Pisces

Energy level Capricorn: October 2024

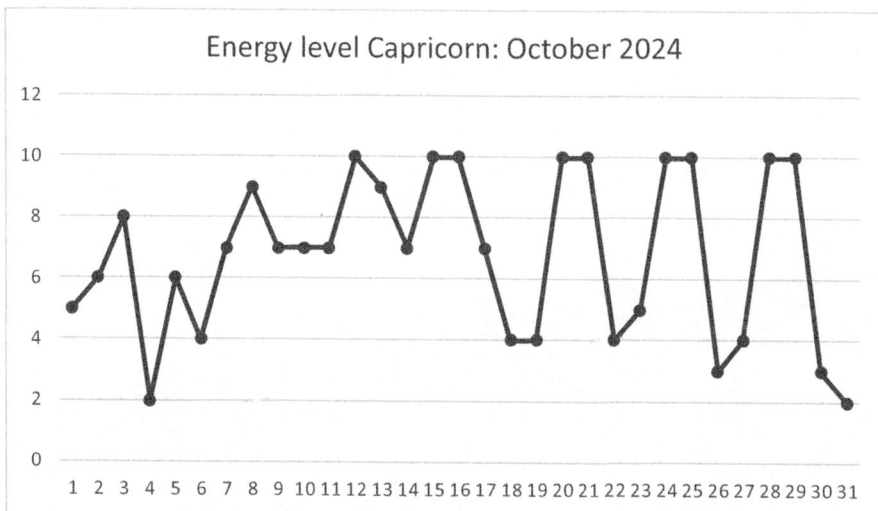

NOVEMBER

💜 *Love* On November 12, Venus moves into your zodiac sign, Capricorn. That's when a powerful, magical constellation forms in the sky, with you at its focal point. The consequences: Storm in love, chances of century encounters, passion, happiness and possibly offspring. Your very best day is November 17. The Venus and the moon meet. Ruth this is a sign for miracles.

🏆 *Success* There exists a small problem: on some days you get nervous quickly and go off the deep end in no time. The reason: you put yourself under too much pressure and would be better off taking a break. Your best time is between November 10 and 20.

👍 *Good for* Luck in love

☹ *Bad for* Not believing in yourself

✦ *Best star partners* Virgo, Cancer, Scorpio, Pisces

Energy level Capricorn: November 2024

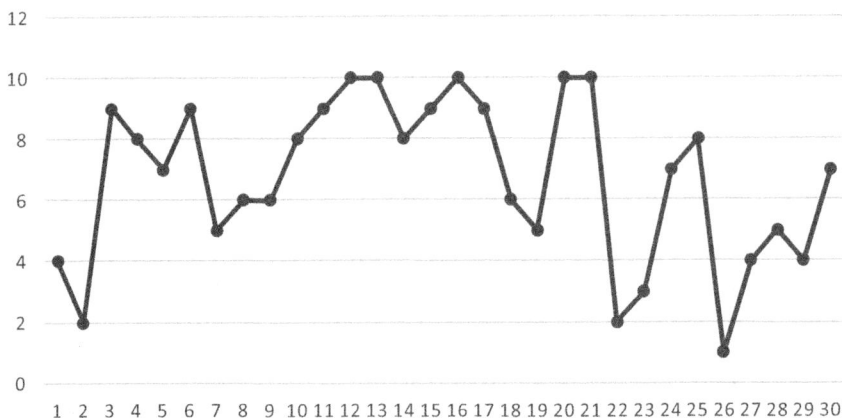

DECEMBER

♥ **Love** Until the end of the year, you can relax, be lazy and enjoy. The stars ensure that you are not alone in this. Your love thermometer may not be sensational, but it's enough for sweet adventures in the realm of the senses. You will be particularly lucky if you take a trip over Christmas. Every kilometer away from home increases your chances with the opposite sex.

♕ **Success** In the job you get a great opportunity to distinguish yourself. But from the middle of the month on all ambition is in vain: Do what has to be done! Otherwise you have to take it easy and eat healthy food rich in vitamins! You are a favorite victim of colds right now. For the Christmas holidays this year, allow yourself a lot of rest and serenity.

👍 **Good for** Thinking positive

☹ **Bad for** Being distrustful

✦ **Best star partners** Capricorn

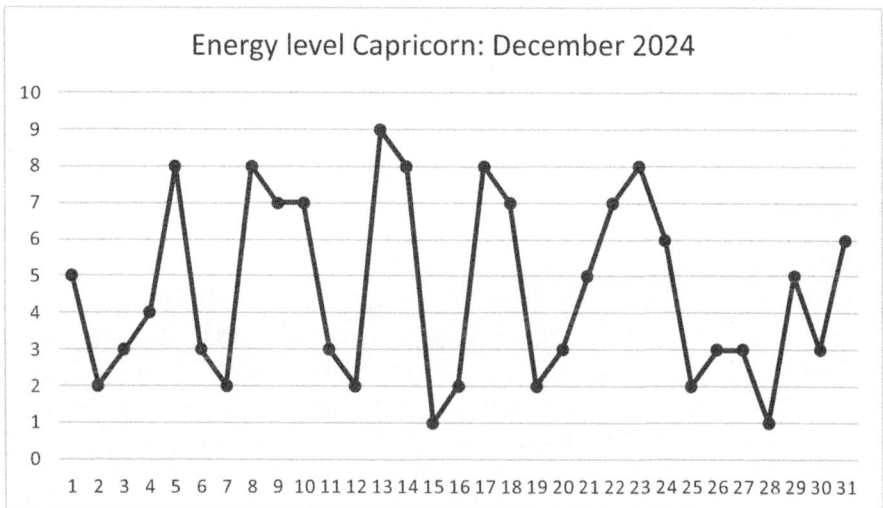

Energy level Capricorn: December 2024

AQUARIUS
(January 21 - February 19)

The sun rules the year. It strengthens your light side. You have not been so well for a long time. It makes you a popular and sought-after person with whom people enjoy spending time and also working together. A lot of good comes from Jupiter, the lucky planet, which is at your side from May 25. What you will have to get used to is Pluto. This planet moves into your zodiac sign Aquarius in January 2024 and stays there for the next fifteen years. By its nature, this planet is the absolute antagonist to you. Because, according to your attitude, what is good should stay and become better and what is worse should pass away. But Pluto doesn't care about the good, it cares about the bad and makes it disappear. The good is to remain. Basically it comes with both to the same, namely a better life, but the way there is different, even downright opposite. Therefore: It will be exciting in the coming year.

What is in store for Aquarians? On the one hand to delete everything from their lives that has no value and is unimportant, on the other hand to promote everything that points positively into the future. In the way you succeed in this, you fulfill your task as an Aquarius. For this you do not have to be active far up, for example, in politics. Every Aquarius, no matter how seemingly unimportant the work they do, contributes in 2024 to how this world goes on and whether it has a future at all.

LOVE
Pluto in your zodiac sign also makes itself felt in your love life. Thanks to the ruler of the year, the Sun, your effect on the opposite sex increases enormously. As a single you may enjoy all this uninhibitedly and experience, if the new conquest pleases you, also more often than usual, a wonderful night together. Whether this will turn into a permanent relationship depends not only on the stars, but also on you. Things look tur-

bulent for Aquarians who are already in firm hands. The reason: They flirt like crazy and that while someone is waiting for them at home. Of course, it can sometimes crackle violently or even crash. In any case, your love life will be fresher, bolder and more daring. Sooner or later Pluto will ask you the question if your love is coherent: Do you profit from each other? Can the positive become stronger, and is the negative weakening? Is it right to stay in this relationship? There are definitely not less Aquarians in 2024 who get out of their partnership because they don't agree with the way things are going. And there are many Aquarians in 2024 who prefer to stay single or are satisfied with a partnership among like-minded people.

Sun, Jupiter, Pluto:
Your mystical year full of possibilities

CAREER

With Sun and from July Jupiter a great duet is on your side. Luck meets you at every turn, but it can't be taken for granted either. You need to mobilize your forces to prove what you can do. Your stars make you more courageous, more inventive, more self-confident in some ways even a bit ingenious. But the discipline needed to keep at it until you reach the goal of something must come from you. For that, you need Saturn. This important star, which was your ruling planet before Uranus was discovered, resides in the zodiac sign of Pisces in 2024. With this, it is not enough if you earn a lot of money, live well, and live well, but if your work makes sense. This coincides with the intention of Pluto, as said before. So in 2024 you can't help but keep asking yourself how meaningful your life is. What you must not forget or repress is that as an Aquarian, you are partly responsible for how our world is going. If you are considering a change of residence or looking for a new job, you should not take action until June. That's when Jupiter is strong. You will have the most power in August and in the second half of November.

CHARACTER:	Free, energetic, progressive
PERSONAL APPEARANCE:	Independent, idealistic
FEELING:	Primal, elemental
STONE:	Amber
ANIMAL:	Parrot
FLOWER:	Orchid
BEST DAY:	Saturday

JANUARY

♥ **Love** The love planet Venus is in the zodiac sign Sagittarius until the 23rd of the month. and conjures a magic that makes miracles possible That you are not simply "only" loved, but also understood. Too good to be true? Maybe! But moments of happiness like these are definitely on the cards for you in January.

♆ **Success** On January 5, Mars moves into the zodiac sign of Capricorn. This will definitely encourage you to make a push in your career: that's right! The stars are nodding, which means you are successful. Be careful at the end of the month: Be very precise!

👍 **Good for** Savoring the opportunities

☹ **Bad for** Self-doubt

✦ **Best star partners** Leo, Libra, Sagittarius

Energy level Aquarius: January 2024

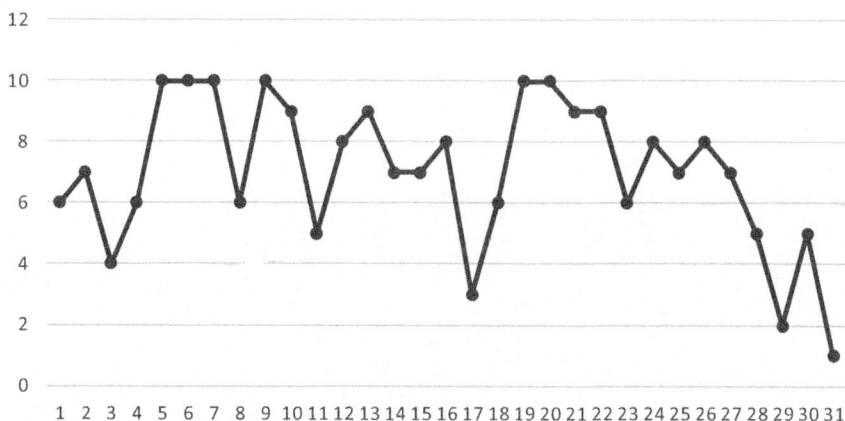

FEBRUARY

Now Pluto is in the zodiac sign Aquarius, where it will stay for almost 20 years. So it's certainly not wrong to get ready for it now: Pluto demands change. It means letting go of habits to make way for something new and better.

💜 *Love* You don't really warm up. Even your birthday party won't break any records. But you might have fun at a carnival party. In the second half of the month your stars look much better for love. Now even small miracles are possible.

For some among you, a pay raise is in the air.

🏆 *Success* In February, don't get carried away with any deal that sounds promising but ultimately yields nothing. In other words, be cautious and, above all, humble.

👍 *Good for* Taking a lot of time for yourself

☹ *Bad for* Indifference

✦ *Best star partners* Aquarius, Leo

Energy level Aquarius: February 2024

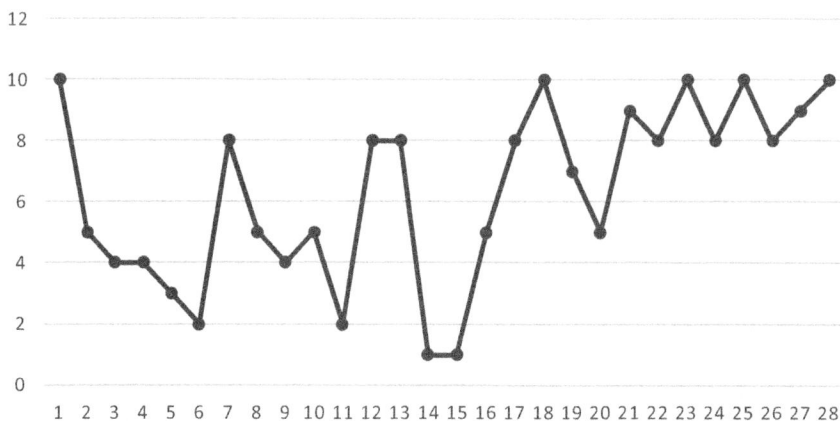

MARCH

💜 **Love** Mars and Venus move together through your sign Aquarius until March 10. This means that entertaining encounters, as well as love and passion, are definitely in the stars. The better prospects, however, are the first two weeks.

🏆 **Success** Things don't look bad here either. Mars and Venus make you inventive. This can easily translate into business. You have to be careful around March 17: Your stars mean that you are quite easily deceived.

👍 **Good for** Green light for an advance in your career.

☹ **Bad for** Letting your courage be taken away

✦ **Best star partners** Aquarius, Gemini, Sagittarius, Leo

Energy level Aquarius: March 2024

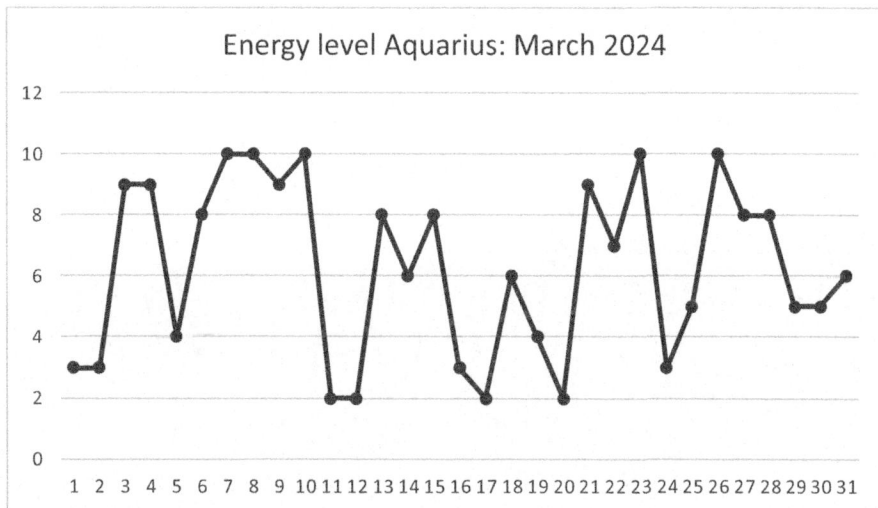

APRIL

💜 *Love* Things are looking good for love in April. Even in relationships that have been battered by the storm over the last few years, peace, quiet and love will now return. Interesting encounters beckon to the singles among you - certainly also with the chance of a partnership. Especially interesting would be a person with the same zodiac sign as yours, i.e. Aquarius

🏆 *Success* You must now take into account that Mars is in the zodiac sign of Pisces and is conjunct Saturn: cleverness and skill are required. You'll do very badly with the "hair-pulling" method. Around the middle of the month you must be ready for a change, even if you don't know how it will turn out.

👍 *Good for* Believing in yourself

☹ *Bad for* Losing heart

✨ *Best star partners* Aquarius, Leo, Aries

Energy level Aquarius: April 2024

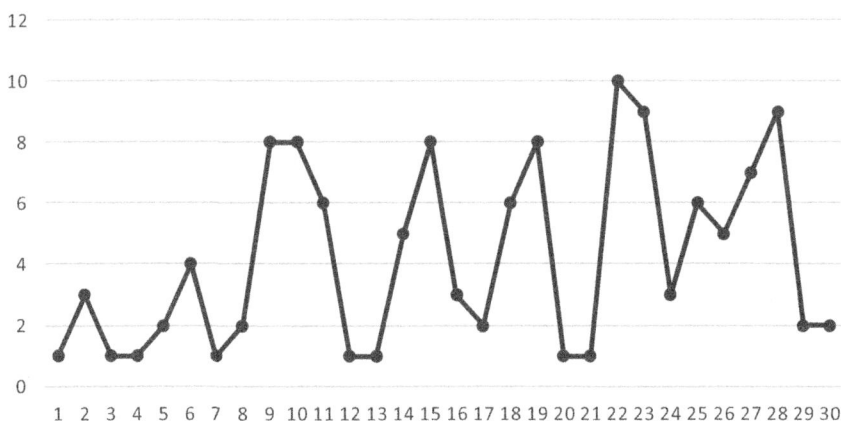

MAY

💜 **Love** Planet Mars drives you. But this is very pleasant, because your life gets momentum. Venus makes sure that you automatically look out for the beautiful. Quite a few among you will thereby meet the person who fits your life. You will be happy. Now lifelong partnerships arise.

🏆 **Success** Until the 20th of the month the sun is in the zodiac sign Taurus. This means that the topic of finances is also at the top of the list.

It is quite possible that you are worried. From the 20th then it gets better, because now the Sun connects with Jupiter and dispels all worries about money. Have confidence!

👍 **Good for** New attitude towards life

☹ **Bad for** Not believing in the good, being pessimistic, resigning.

✦ **Best star partners** Aquarius, Leo

Energy level Aquarius: May 2024

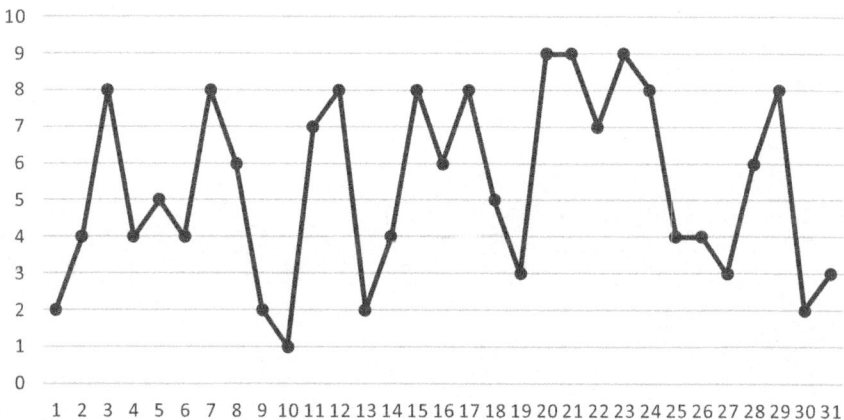

179

JUNE

💜 **Love** You need a person who is strong and motivated like you. This may also mean one day that you leave the person you are living with now because he is not a match for you. Then you will get a new partner. If you are single, you will find a person who is the right one. With him you will master your task. Together you will climb to the top.

🏆 **Success** Jupiter, Mercury, the Sun and Venus are opposite your zodiac sign. Thus, this month has great potential. You will bring forth something. There is significance in you. You can find a new position at work that is much better than your current one.

👍 **Good for** Believing in yourself

☹ **Bad for** Not dealing with the past. Closing oneself off.

✦ **Best star partners** Leo, Gemini, Sagittarius

Energy level Aquarius: June 2024

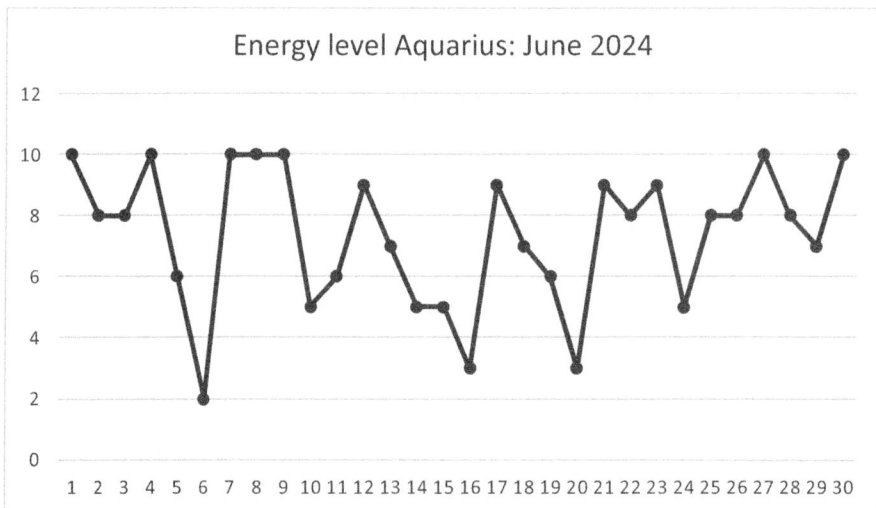

JULY

💜 *Love* As far as love is concerned, until the 20th of the month, the Sun and Venus guarantee a superlative time. The affairs are sweet and the associated partners charming, sensitive, eager to commit, but not sticky. Conclusion: a love life like out of a picture book. On the last ten days of July it will be very nice even without love.

🏆 *Success* Lucky planet Jupiter, takes a fantastic position in July. It clears hurdles and obstacles out of the way. For those of you who are waiting for career improvement, this Jupiter will definitely be a help. You can become happy. Trust your future destiny!

👍 *Good for* Love that makes you happy

☹ *Bad for* Being too critical

✨ *Best star partners* Leo

Energy level Aquarius: July 2024

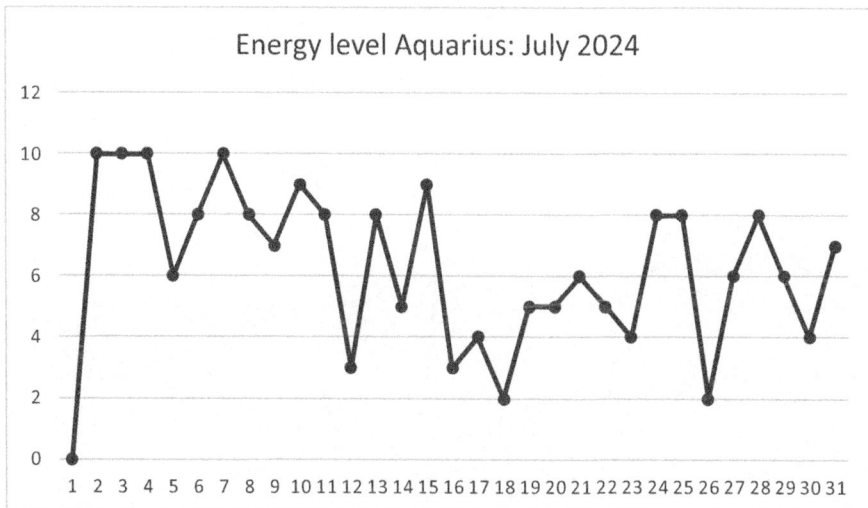

181

AUGUST

💜 **Love** The Sun, regent of the year and also of the month of August, gives you love for yourself. Friendships benefit as well as firm partnerships. Your relationship with each other becomes more mature, deeper, more enduring. Singles also go through life full of life. Fixed relationship? Oh God, how stuffy! After all, it's possible without commitment.

🏆 **Success** In August you need more breaks. An Aquarius, who works permanently too much, then is also in the spare time sore as active, brings in the long run nothing more. Call it what you want: a cuddle, honeymoon.

👍 **Good for** Luck

☹ **Bad for** Being intemperate

✦ **Best star partners** Aquarius, Aries, Leo

Energy level Aquarius: August 2024

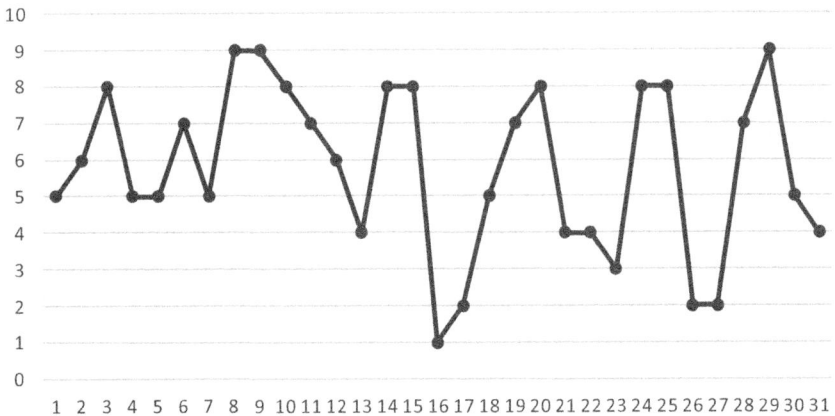

SEPTEMBER

💜 **Love** The love planet Venus is in a friendly trine to your star sign. Even inveterate singles long for a partner and are willing to give up freedom and independence. There are plenty of opportunities in September. Couples are also sure of love. You invest a lot and spoil your partner.

🏆 **Success** Pluto, the great transformer, is in your zodiac sign and brings out hidden talents, tickles awake potentials that lie dormant in you. You will change and be amazed at your resources. Magic? coincidence? Fate? Call it what you will. The main thing is that you are grateful that new possibilities exist.

👍 **Good for** Planning the future

☹ **Bad for** Pessimism

✦ **Best star partners** Leo, Aquarius

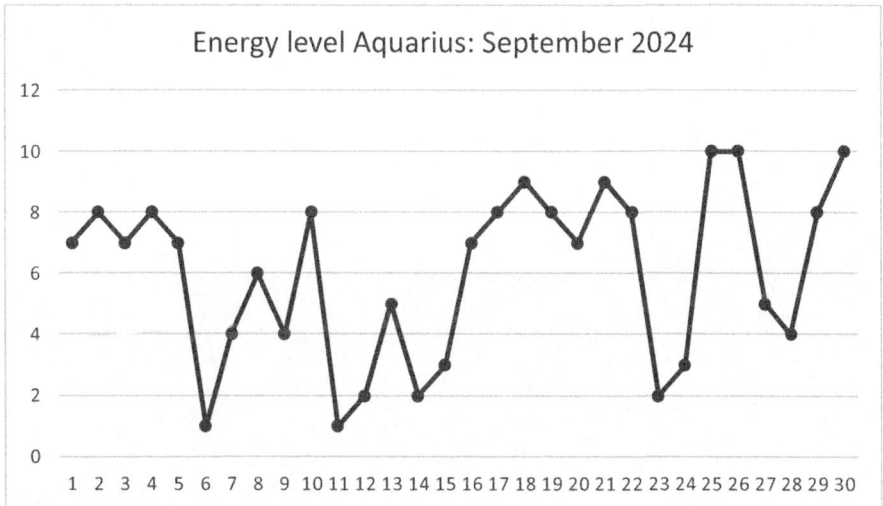

Energy level Aquarius: September 2024

OCTOBER

💜 **Love** The way your stars are positioned, you can easily deceive yourself in October. You'd be well advised to use your head and distrust your feelings. Don't worry, it's not a big story, but if you keep that in mind, it will be easier, and you certainly won't make a mistake.

🏆 **Success** There will be nothing about casually twiddling your thumbs in October. Your career demands everything. Keep up with it, then you can laugh at the end! There is one extra hint: The stars indicate that you cannot rely on friends unconditionally in October.

👍 **Good for** Reason

☹ **Bad for** Ingratitude

✦ **Best star partners** Leo, Libra

Energy level Aquarius: October 2024

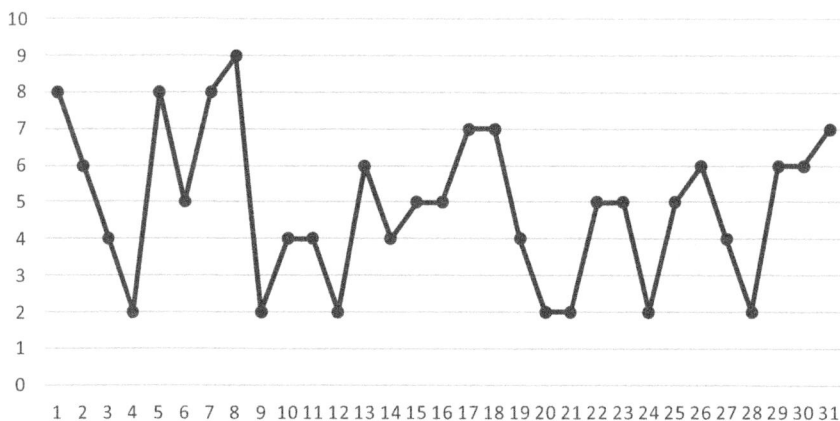

NOVEMBER

💜 **Love** From the middle of the month, planet Mars provides hearts and thus promising prospects in love. Even that is possible for a chance encounter to turn into a hot love story. Tell your heart to be open by all means.

🏆 **Success** In November many things work out if you are with yourself - and little if you lose your center. Pause more often, take your time and collect yourself! This is especially true for the new moon phase around the 1st of the month. For days after that you will still be flabby and easily fragile. From the 20th, the stars provide you with a strong end of the month.

👍 **Gut für** Founding a family

☹ **Bad for** Boredom

✦ **Best star partners** Scorpio, Pisces, Aquarius

Energy level Aquarius: November 2024

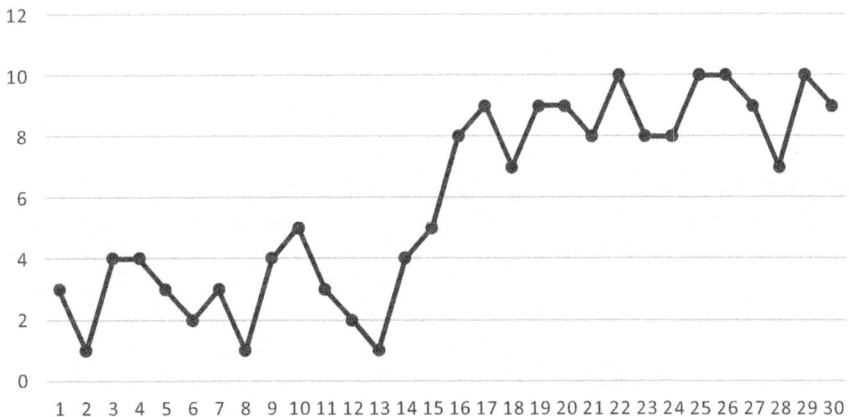

DECEMBER

♥ **Love** Sex planet Mars moves into a favorable position. From lively -spiritual flirtations to inspiring nights, everything is in it, and you combine everything a person needs to be desirable: Charisma, self-confidence and nonchalance. Now love just has to work out

♕ **Success** You are the most successful zodiac sign of the ent- ire month. Promotions, raises, and expansions of your sphere of influence are literally in the air. The best time to make a push in the personnel office or at your bank is during the week beginning December 7.

👍 **Gut für** Great satisfaction

☹ **Bad for** Modesty

✦ **Best star partners** Aquarius, Libra, Gemini

Energy level Aquarius: December 2024

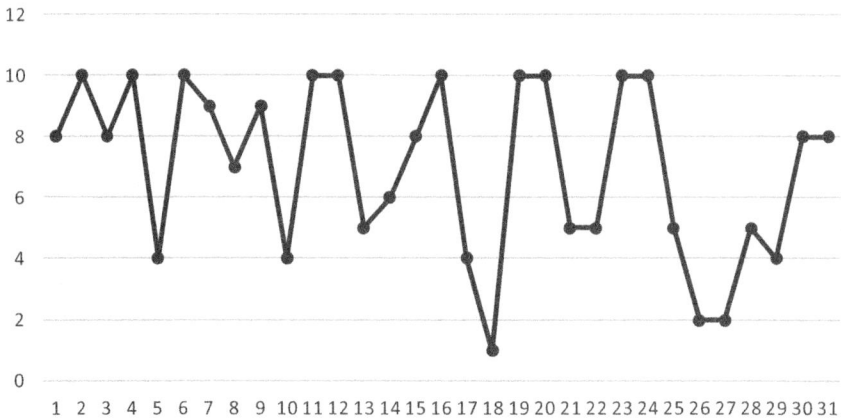

Coupon
10 EURO

FOR BUYING THIS BOOK

EARN BACK

YOUR VOUCHER CODE FOR 10 EURO DISCOUNT

FOR YOUR

PERSONAL HOROSCOPE:

Horoscope2024

ORDERS ARE ACCEPTED IN THE SHOP
WWW.ASTROPORTAL.COM/SHOP. IN THIS SHOP YOU CAN ALSO
REDEEM THE VOUCHER FOR ANY HOROSCOPE. THIS VOUCHER IS
VALID UNTIL 31 DECEMBER 2024.

How does it work?

Your personal future: It doesn't get any truer than this!
As a thank you for purchasing this book, you will receive the purchase price of the book as a discount for the creation of your personal annual horoscope. Star astrologer Erich Bauer will be happy to analyze your personal stars. You will receive your personal annual horoscope for 12 months plus one bonus month for free.
Take a look at the next 12 months with your personal annual horoscope. For all orders there is an additional bonus of a 13th month free of charge with your future forecast by Erich Bauer incl. film message.
You will receive this bonus in two variants of future analyses from which you can choose:

Variant 1: Proven bonus annual horoscope as PDF or as printed book for only EUR 39.90 (length approx. 40 pages) delivered in 5 analysis parts individually created for you.

Variant 2: Bonus Annual Horoscope Premium. There is probably no more accurate forecast of the future in Germany than the Annual Horoscope Premium. If you want to take a detailed look at your personal future.

https://www.astroportal.com/shop

Printed in Great Britain
by Amazon